A WALK IN THE LIFE
Lessons From God's People

"My Time with God Collection"

A WALK IN THE LIFE
Lessons From God's People

"My Time with God Collection"

Dr. Jewel D. Williams

Where we Publish the Vision

Helping people WIN in Publishing

A WALK IN THE LIFE

Copyright © 2022 by Dr. Jewel D. Williams

ISBN-13:979-8-9868609-1-6

All Rights Reserved. No part of this publication may be reproduced, stored in any retrieval system, or transmitted in any form or by any means, electronic, mechanical, photocopy, recording, or any other, except for brief quotations in printed reviews, without the prior, written permission of the author.

For more information or to order additional copies, please contact the publisher.

Tri-Production Publishing, Inc.
C/O Dr. Jewel D. Williams
P.O. Box 198698
Chicago, IL 60619
Drjewelwilliams@publishthevision.com

Table of Contents

INTRODUCTION	1
A BETTER WAY	2
HOLD ONTO THE FAITH	13
A PARENT'S HEART	24
THE INCREASE	36
UNUSUAL ASSIGNMENTS	47
FIRST THINGS FIRST	60
THE OFFENSE	71
CHARACTER ON DISPLAY	83
THE UNNAMED MOTHER	94
THE MESSAGE	106

INTRODUCTION

     A Walk in the Life is a collection of my personal studies based on people from the Bible. These were ordinary people doing extraordinary things. It is through this study that I found affirmation that we are all called to live for God no matter where we've come from or what we think we are capable of doing.

     Each of the lives portrayed in the Bible reminds us of our flaws, our strengths and our ability to trust in God. I hope you find encouragement on the pages of this book as you walk through the life of some of God's people. In fact, on this journey you may find yourself.

     A Walk in the Life is the third book in my series, *My Time With God Collection.* Other books in the *My Time with God Collection* are available. Living Our Theology and In His Name – The Attributes of God, are the first two in this series.

God bless,
Apostle Dr. Jewel D. Williams
Lead pastors of Vision and Education
Abundant Life Worship Center

A BETTER WAY

APOSTLE PAUL was first introduced to us in Acts 7:57-58 NLT where it states, "Then they put their hands over their ears and began shouting. They rushed at him and dragged him out of the city and began to stone him. His accusers took off their coats and laid them at the feet of a young man named Saul." Paul, then Saul was at the killing of Stephen. Chapter 8:1 NLT states, "Saul was one of the witnesses, and he agreed completely with the killing of Stephen." Not necessarily a good entrance into a story, is it? But how many of us can say our beginning was stellar?

As we continue to read about Paul, he was in pursuit of destroying the church (Acts 8:3). From the beginning, Paul doesn't appear to be someone who would be used by God, especially since his pursuit was to destroy those who followed after Christ. Yet, God sees our usefulness differently than how we see others. We determine another's past can disqualify them from future usefulness; that's not God's way. Paul's life reminds us that it doesn't matter how we start, but that we submit our lives to be used for God's purpose.

While in pursuit of destroying those who followed after Christ, Paul had an encounter with Christ (Acts 9:1-31), the one he believed was dead. This man, Saul, with such rage against the followers of Christ was about to become one of Christianity's greatest apostles. Saul's name was changed to Paul and he began his life as a believer filled with vigor and power. This same man who was determined to stop the spread of Christianity was now in pursuit of telling all that would listen about Christ.

As we walk through the life of Paul, he offers us some very practical steps to ensure we present the Gospel to all people, encouraging us to be accessible, without changing the truth of the word.

A Walk With the Apostle Paul – Paul and the Law

> Yet we know that a person is made right with God by faith in Jesus Christ, not by obeying the law. And we have believed in Christ Jesus, so that we might be made right with God because of our faith in Christ, not because we have obeyed the law. For no one will ever be made right with God by obeying the law." – **Galatians 2:16 NLT**

Paul was educated and studied under the ranking rabbi of the era, Gamaliel I. Paul's use of the Old Testament bears testimony to his rabbinic training. Paul preached and taught against the polytheism belief of his time. He taught there was only one God. He preached that God was personal and accessible rather than impersonal. Against most pagan religions, Paul presented a God concerned with social morality and personal ethics. His teaching affirmed that God is to be feared, loved, served and worshiped. Paul was not directing others to himself, but to the one true God.

Here, Paul warns against the snare of believing in self-salvation by law-keeping alone. Remember, this is the same one who was determined to kill and imprison anyone who was teaching what he was now holding as truth. He believed completely in the keeping of the Law, yet because he discovered a better way, he now teaches the Scripture more completely. Our lesson from Paul is we should always be willing to have our own beliefs strengthened and checked by God to make sure we are aligned with truth and not stuck in religious ideas.

During Paul's time some were trying to insist that circumcision and the keeping of certain Jewish customs had to be done but Paul was teaching that it is not by the keeping of the law that one is saved, but by faith in *Jesus alone*. He is not, however, saying not to be obedient to the things of God, but simply it is not in our works that we are justified.

This has caused much confusion regarding what Paul was really saying. Yet, I believe it is clear. He is telling those of his day, as well as us today that we are not saved by our own works. In today's language we would say, "I'm a good person, I don't steal, I don't lie, I go to church, I tithe, etc., so I should be able to go to heaven". While that may be a true fact (all relevant to what or who you are comparing yourself to), it is not in our own goodness that salvation is received. Salvation comes only through Christ. Paul reminds us about this truth and we are encouraged to be obedient to the things of God so that we can live a life that God is calling us to live. Paul prompts us to be vested in our relationship with Christ to be capable of doing the things of God.

> "For I am not ashamed of the gospel of Christ: for it is the power of God unto salvation to every one that believeth; to the Jew first, and also to the Greek. For therein is the righteousness of God revealed from faith to faith: as it is written, The just shall live by faith. For the wrath of God is revealed from heaven against all ungodliness and unrighteousness of men, who hold the truth in unrighteousness; Because that which may be known of God is manifest in them; for God hath shown *it* unto them." – **Romans 1:16-19 KJV**

Paul's epistle to the Roman church has power that can still touch lives today. Martin Luther stated his life was changed after reading the book of Romans. Luther said he pondered night and day how a sinner like himself could ever stand forgiven before God who is perfectly righteous and will one day judge everyone.

Just as Martin Luther was able to find comfort in Romans, so can we. Paul boldly states, he is not ashamed of the gospel of Christ. He is not afraid to tell others about it. He is not afraid of the persecution that may come because of it. Why is he not afraid? I believe he isn't afraid because he remembers his personal conversion. He remembers going from being an enemy of Christ to one saved by His gift of love. When a person remembers their conversion story, it makes for a powerful resolve to withstand whatever could happen to them as a result of their belief. It is our faith *in* Christ that will help us to grow *in* our faith walk.

Paul was speaking to those that were faced with a culture that was not receptive of the good news. Paul also warns his listeners that those who reject the gift revealed by God to mankind would in fact receive the wrath of God. There is no question about it; Christ is the way chosen by God for redemption of all mankind. If we do not accept it, it does not matter how good we think we are or how good we think our deeds are, we will suffer the wrath of God.

Paul boldly gives this message. It wasn't one well received then, and it isn't today. Yet, Paul was willing to face the backlash for preaching the good news about faith. As followers of Christ, we must be determined that everyone won't like the message but we must be like Paul and give it anyway.

A Walk With the Apostle Paul – Paul and God's Wrath

> "For the wrath of God is revealed from heaven against all ungodliness and unrighteousness of men who suppress the truth in unrighteousness, because that which is known about God is evident within them; for God made it evident to them. For since the creation of the world His invisible attributes, His eternal power and divine nature, have been clearly seen, being understood through what has been made, so that they are without excuse. For even though they knew God, they did not honor Him as God or

give thanks, but they became futile in their speculations, and their foolish heart was darkened. Professing to be wise, they became fools, and exchanged the glory of the incorruptible God for an image in the form of corruptible man and of birds and four-footed animals and crawling creatures." – **Romans 1:18-23 KJV**

Paul is attempting to show the need of the Gospel to both the Gentiles as well as the Jews in this letter to the Roman church. In these verses Paul says that the wrath of God is revealed against all ungodliness and unrighteousness. Paul starts with the Gentiles. He tells them there are those who have evidence of God through creation. From the beginning of this world, God was showing His attributes to all who had eyes to see them. God showed His power and divine nature clearly. Therefore, no one has any excuses to ignore Him. Yet, men did not honor God and they did not give thanks for His provisions. Instead they began to worship created things instead of the creator.

This is a vital point for us today. God still makes Himself evident in our world. If we look around we can see the mountains, the birds that fly, the newborn baby and marvel at the fact there has to be something greater than ourselves behind these wonders. Yet, we refuse to acknowledge God, instead we take credit for the things in our world. We believe it's because of our own doing and wisdom. Nevertheless, Paul calls those types of people fools. We become foolish in our own wisdom when we refuse to acknowledge God.

Paul highlights man's wickedness to help them realize no one can stand before God without help. Furthermore, he states no one will have an excuse for their rejection of God. Paul wasn't speaking from a place of judgment, but I submit he is speaking from a place of understanding. He was foolish before he accepted salvation through Christ. He wasn't acknowledging Christ as Savior. He was doing just the opposite; he was trying to stop those who were believers in Christ.

Paul's encouragement for us is to make sure we aren't foolish in our understanding about God and His plans. We must seek God, even in the everyday things to allow us to see Him more clearly. And this will allow us to walk in the Spirit led life.

A Walk With the Apostle Paul – Paul and the Spirit led Life

> "Be not deceived; God is not mocked: for whatsoever a man soweth, that shall he also reap. For he that soweth to his flesh shall of the flesh reap corruption; but he that soweth to the Spirit shall of the Spirit reap life everlasting. And let us not be weary in well doing: for in due season we shall reap, if we faint not. As we have therefore opportunity, let us do good unto all *men*, especially unto them who are of the household of faith" – **Galatians 6:7-10 KJV**

Paul's letter to the Galatians puts the focus on freedom from a performance-based approach to pleasing God. Paul is disturbed because the Galatians' churches seem on the verge of falling away from the faith Paul preached to them (Gal. 5:4). He was warning the Galatians not to be fooled by false teachers that are teaching that it is work (by one's own hands) that salvation is received. Paul continually reminds his audience that it is by grace and not human merit we are saved.

In the nineteenth century a social gospel spread. The preaching of Christ's cross was replaced by social work activities, educational, economic, and political strategies. The greatest held belief was that salvation could be obtained by helping others. While all of these are important to the individual, they are not the way of salvation. They can help the human condition but they do not save the soul. This message from Paul should ring again in our hearing. Let us not be deceived. We are to always make the message of salvation our first offer to those we encounter. And in that pursuit, we should not get weary because the things we do for Christ will last.

Paul further encourages the reader to do good unto all men. Paul is telling us it is important to be concerned about the needs of others (especially the household of faith), but nowhere does he tell us that we are to use this social gospel to replace the gospel of Christ. We need to continue to hear Christ's cross preached for the saving of the people. And from the cross message we also seek ways to help people become good citizens, fathers, mothers and more. The cross is the main message, not an afterthought or replaced by a lesser gospel. The message Paul is preaching is for us to follow after God. In that pursuit, God calls us to give the message to others as we also seek to help them in their everyday lives.

A Walk With the Apostle Paul – Paul and the Truth

> "Having a form of godliness, but denying the power thereof: from such turn away. For of this sort are they which creep into houses, and lead captive silly women laden with sins, led away with divers lusts, Ever learning, and never able to come to the knowledge of the truth." – **2 Timothy 3:5-17 KJV**

It is believed that shortly after writing 2 Timothy, Paul apparently suffered death by beheading under persecutions instigated by the degenerated madness of the Roman emperor Nero. However, Paul never stopped sharing the truth, even from prison. He didn't allow his situation or circumstances to keep him from his pursuit of godly things.

Here, Paul warns Timothy about the things he should be concerned about in the church. Paul warned about the false teachers that would threaten the stability and integrity of the Christian community. Paul reminds Timothy on what things he should focus on, prayer and worship. Paul further warns Timothy about those who have a form of godliness but deny the true power. He says they are always learning but never actually grasping the truth. This was an admonition Paul continued to give again and again, to be careful of false doctrine and vain babblings.

There are people today who believe that all the world religions contain truth about God and there isn't one right way. Paul in his teachings was facing these types of beliefs of his time. He was warning the people to be careful of those things that sound good, yet they deny the truth of God. They are forever trying to learn, but in their learning, they are not getting wiser, but are in fact becoming blinded.

Life Lessons

Paul's beginning shows us how deeply entrenched he was in the Jewish faith. He thought he was doing something good and honorable in trying to eliminate those who followed after Christ. However, God showed Him a better way when he met Christ on the road to Damascus. Some of us need a Damascus road experience to have our belief systems challenged. Things we think are good, God will show us are actually standing in the way of us walking fully in the path He has for us.

Paul stood in the face of prison and other things that should have made him quit. Paul reminds us we need to have a "no quit" attitude. We must be willing to face rejection and being unpopular. In fact, popularity shouldn't even be something we seek after. Paul told the truth. And as we know truth isn't always welcomed, but we should tell it anyway.

Paul reminds us to keep first things first. The message of the cross, and Christ crucified for the saving of souls, has to be our foundational message. We can't make personal comforts, or riches, or anything else more important than the cross. We start with the cross and from there we share how Christ allows us to do other things, like helping in the social arena. We learn how to make the cross available to all men for all reasons; that's how we become all things to all men to show them a better way.

HOLD ONTO THE FAITH

APOSTLE JOHN is the writer of the Fourth Gospel as well as the three New Testament books named after him. This John is the son of Zebedee, and the "beloved disciple" of Christ. Acts 8-12 counts John as one of the individuals prominent in the rise and growth of the church. John was sent with Peter by the Jerusalem church to Samaria to confirm the believers (Acts 8).

Our early introduction to John was with the other disciples. We saw they often didn't understand as a whole Christ's instructions. They were looking for an earthly kingdom but Christ was talking about a spiritual one. While the disciples didn't always understand the full magnitude of Christ's message, we see John stayed true to teaching and sharing the Gospel.

John isn't much different than many of us. We think we understand the things of God, but sometimes discover our understanding is limited. That inadequacy can be based on our expectations or what we want. But even our limitations don't have to keep us from walking in the fullness of who we are called to be. John was able to gain a fuller understanding. It is from that place he shares and teaches others. We should do likewise.

A Walk With the Apostle John – John's Warning

> "That which was from the beginning, which we have heard, which we have seen with our eyes, which we have looked upon, and our hands have handled, of the Word of life: (For the life was manifested, and we have seen it, and bear witness, and show unto you that eternal life, which was manifested unto us;) That which we have seen and heard declare we unto you, that ye also may have fellowship with us; and truly our fellowship is with the Father, and with his Son Jesus Christ. And these things write we unto you, that your joy may be full." – **1 John 1:1-4 KJV**

John was concerned with the Gnostic philosophy that was creeping into the Christian faith. The opinion was Christ only appeared to have a body but didn't really have one. The opinion of the time was that the deeds we do with our bodies which are inherently evil, cannot contaminate our souls, which are inherently good. This belief fueled the stand that Jesus couldn't have been in a body because of its inherent evil. John was addressing these beliefs.

In these verses John begins by telling his audience why he is writing. He says he is writing so that their joy may be full in the knowledge that Jesus is the Son of God who *has* appeared in the flesh. He immediately addresses the confusion about Jesus not having a body. John informs his listeners God himself dwells in us if we confess that

Jesus is the Son of God (1 John 4:15). John was encouraging his audience to stand strong in the truth which they had already been given.

John was trying to strengthen the believers not to allow the truth to be taken away from them by popular beliefs. When people come to change the way of God, we must reject it. The Bible clearly states to us what Jesus did and why He did it. Jesus came to save sinful men. He came because the sinful deeds done in the body have sentenced the soul to hell. If we do not accept the gift of salvation that Christ came to give, we will be held accountable for our actions done in this body. Let no one fool you! This is what John was telling in his epistle.

John was encouraging his listeners that it was vital to fight for and hold on to God's truth. John understood the importance of gaining a fuller understanding of biblical truth. When we were first saved, we accepted the truth of God's word. We must not allow the world to come and snatch away that which we know to be true.

John also reminds us that we can grow and expand our understanding about God and His plan for us and humanity as a whole. Remember, he wasn't always clear about Jesus' teaching. But he had to be willing to keep learning and allowing God's Spirit to build faith in him. That's the same for us today. It's okay that we didn't understand fully in the beginning, but we must be responsible for our development and growth by studying and seeking God daily.

A Walk With the Apostle John – John Gives the Message

> "This then is the message which we have heard of him, and declare unto you, that God is light, and in him is no darkness at all. If we say that we have fellowship with him, and walk in darkness, we lie, and do not the truth: But if we walk in the light as he is in the light, we have fellowship one with another, and the blood of Jesus Christ his Son cleanseth us from all sin. If we say we have no sin, we deceive ourselves, and the truth is not in us. If we confess our sins, he is faithful and just to forgive us our sins, and to cleanse us from all unrighteousness. If we say that we have not sinned, we make him a liar, and his word is not in us." – **1 John 1:5-10 KJV**

John continues to remind his audience of the message they were given. The message is God is light and when we have fellowship with Him, He is the one that will keep us through whatever we face in life. If we do not do what is right, we then are liars. We say we are believers yet if our actions and decisions do not reflect this, then where is the light? Have we made ourselves liars because what we say isn't aligned with how we live?

The second part of this Scripture gives us an important message. If we say that we never have sinned and have nothing to seek forgiveness for, we are deceiving ourselves. Yet if we are willing to seek God daily for the things in our lives which need to be changed, He is faithful to forgive us. I'd like to point something out here. Before we became believers we were sinners and totally lost. When we accepted God's gift of salvation, we moved from being sinners separated from God to children of God. Yet, it is imperative that we seek God daily to make sure we bring all our actions under subjection to the direction of the Holy Spirit. In other words, we were saved but our mindset, actions or behaviors had not yet been fully transformed.

We never want to think that because we are under grace that the sin that dwells in our lives is okay. God is seeking us to transform into the image of His Son. Our lives should be in line with what we profess with our mouths. If we say we are children of God, then our actions should reflect that.

John shows us the importance of understanding the message of salvation for ourselves but also as we share it with others. We also need to make sure that as we walk out our salvation we allow our lives to be what draws others to Christ.

A Walk With the Apostle John – John Calls all to Holiness

> "My Little children, these things write I unto you, that ye sin not. And if any man sin, we have an advocate with the Father, Jesus Christ the righteous: And he is the propitiation for our sins: and not for ours only, but also for *the sins of* the whole world. And hereby we do know that we know him, if we keep his commandments." – **1 John 2:1-3 KJV**

We get a glimpse from John's words about his heart for the people. He calls them "my little children". As a parent your children are dear to your heart and you want the best for them. John wants the best for God's children as he gives them the truth.

John is not providing his audience some new thing, but a reminder of what they had been given before. He basically tells them, do not sin. The children of God have been given the grace and mercy of God, yet it has not been given for us to misuse. John tells his audience if you do sin, do not stay in that place. Instead we must come to God and present our sins to the one who will be an advocate for us, that is Jesus Christ. And we need to remember that there are those who need to know their sins can be forgiven through Jesus Christ our savior.

God calls for a holy people. The simplest way to understand what holiness looks like, is given in the last verse of John's message. A holy person is one that keeps God's ways. If we do not know what they are, then the Bible holds all we need. If we do not understand them, then we study, seek God's understanding through prayer and the Holy Spirit will teach us. One of the roles of the Holy Spirit in our lives is to teach us. And when we talk about us keeping God's commandments, we aren't talking about trying to stick to the 613 commandments in the Old Testament. We are speaking about following the instructions that Jesus gave us, loving God and loving each other. John's admonition to us is to seek to be obedient to God and not to take advantage of the grace we have to continue to sin.

> "He that saith, I know him, and keepeth not his commandments is a liar, and the truth is not in him. But whoso keepeth his word, in him verily is the love of God perfected: hereby know we that we are in him. He that saith he abideth in him ought himself also so to walk, even as he walked. Brethren, I write no new commandment unto you, but an old commandment which ye had from the beginning. The old commandment is the word which ye have heard from the beginning." – **1 John 2:4-7 KJV**

John continues to remind his audience of what they had been taught. He says to them, if you say you know Him (God) but do not keep His ways, you are a liar and the truth of God is not in you. That sounds like a harsh statement, but John was telling them the importance of doing what God calls us to do.

If we keep the word of God then His love is being perfected in us. We are not perfect, but we are in the process of perfection. In this process our behavior, attitudes, and lifestyles are being made more and more like Christ. So if we say we are abiding in God then it should be evident in the way we live.

John says to his audience, this is not something new that I am telling you. This is an old commandment. What is that old commandment? 2 John 5 also says the same thing, "…that we love one another". God calls for us to love Him and then to love each other. John is reminding his audience of the importance of keeping these commandments.

John repeated himself with verse 4. This is the same thing he said in chapter 1 verse 6 "if we say that we have fellowship with him, and walk in darkness, we lie, and do not the truth". When a point is repeated it isn't just to be redundant, but to get this vital message across. God is calling all that say they love Him to actively live it. We affirm this when our life choices and attitudes show it. Prove it with your service and commitment. Otherwise, we are simply lying to ourselves as well as God.

Jesus did not come to change the law but He came to fulfill it. This is why we don't try to keep all 613 Laws, instead we seek to follow Jesus. Jesus gave instructions for how we should live and if anyone comes and changes that, we are not to follow after it. Even if angels came and gave a different gospel than the one preached, do not follow. Let us hear clearly John's reminder to us of what God is calling for us to do.

John's admonition is for us to remember to trust our lives to Christ. Not to try and do good things in our own power, but to trust the power of God at work in us through Christ. He wants us to remember.

"He that loveth his brother abideth in the light, and there is none occasion of stumbling in him. But he that hateth his brother is in darkness, and walketh in darkness, and knoweth not whither he goeth, because that darkness hath blinded his eyes. I write unto you, little children, because your sins are forgiven you for his name's sake." – **1 John 2:10-12 KJV**

John has repeated this message several times and in several ways. Again the question is why? I have come to understand that sometimes we do not hear instruction given to us the first time, and it needs to be repeated. Especially something that is vitally important must be repeated for the hearer to understand.

So this is what John does. He repeats this message that he gave in the first chapter. That message is if we love our brothers and sisters in Christ, we are living in the light of Christ. And because of it, we are able to walk in the right way. Yet, if we hate our brother or sister we are not walking in the light of Christ but are in darkness. And if you have ever walked into a room without light, you really do not know where you are going or what is in front of you. The darkness has blinded your vision. You are not able to see.

John also reminds them, I am writing to you because this does not have to be. You are saved and your sins have been forgiven so you should be walking in the newness of life that Christ came to bring. Let us remember the message John is trying to convey. How we treat each other is of great importance to our walk with the Lord. We can say all the right things and use all the "holy words" we want to, but when it comes to action, if we do not love each other, we are not following Christ. My prayer is for us to move into action and be doers of what God calls for us to do: love him first and then love each other.

Life Lessons

John considered himself the disciple that Christ loved. I believe we too should see ourselves in that way. Not because we are better, but because we are loved. And then from that place of love we should remember to offer that same love to those we encounter. We must be active in our walk; actively presenting God's love, the same love we have received. This isn't a new commandment, but one God has been drawing us to from the beginning to love Him and others.

John's letters tell his reader why he is writing. We see he was writing to make sure they were full of joy in their knowledge of God. He tells them it was also to make sure they would not sin (2:1). He also wrote to remind them to love one another. John mentions why he has written to them thirteen times (verse 1 John 1:4; 1 John 2:1, 7, 12-14, 21, 26; 1 John 5:13). This is evident that John was concerned about their development in Christ.

John's letter should encourage us to be diligent in our pursuit to obey God, live as an example to others and actively show our love for one another. We also see the importance of staying true to our assignments. John, like Paul, may not have started well, but that doesn't mean he didn't commit to spreading the truth.

John's admonition to all believers is to remember who you have faith in and then walk it out. This isn't some new revelation–it has been God's plan for humanity since the beginning–love God and each other. It was important enough for John to write about it and it's important for us to live it out daily.

A PARENT'S HEART

HANNAH is the mother to the prophet Samuel. In this part of the Scripture he has not yet been born. We are first being introduced to Hannah as she grieves because she desires a child that she doesn't have. She is tormented because she is childless. A woman at this time is expected to provide her husband with a child. Maybe you can relate to Hannah because you expected something that didn't manifest and it made you doubt your purpose.

Yet, as we follow Hannah's story we will learn some things vital for our lives and for those we have been given the honor to parent or lead. Hannah deals with not only the lack of a child but with the taunting of the other wife for her lack. Have you ever had to deal with the taunting of others about your lack? Even if that taunting wasn't intentional, it still felt like a slap in the face because you couldn't do what others were able to do. Hannah addresses for us how we should handle the taunts of our enemies.

A Walk With Hannah – Why Me?

> Now there was a certain man of Ramathaim-zophim, of mount Ephraim, and his name was Elkanah. The son of Jeroham, the son of Elihu, the son of Tohu, the son of Zuph, an Ephrathite: And he had two wives; the name of

the one was Hannah, and the name of the other Peninnah: and Peninnah had children, but Hannah had no children. And this man went up out of his city yearly to worship and to sacrifice unto the LORD of hosts in Shiloh. And the two sons of Eli, Hophni and Phinehas, the Priests of the LORD, were there. And when the time was that Elkanah offered, he gave to Peninnah his wife, and to all her sons and her daughters, portions, but unto Hannah he gave a worthy portion; for he loved Hannah; but the LORD had shut up her womb. – **1 Samuel 1:1-5 KJV**

There was a man who had two wives, Peninnah and Hannah. Peninnah had children but Hannah had none. Hannah had much to be thankful for, she was well loved by her husband as the Scripture tells us, but this was just not enough for Hannah.

For her to be a woman at that time without a child was no simple thing, it was something she was expected to do, give her husband a child, especially a son. We have seen others in Scripture that have been in this same situation. Sarah was one. Abraham loved her but she felt rejection because she did not have a child. As this Scripture unfolds, we will see the difference in how Hannah handles it over how Sarah did. Sarah tried to handle it herself when she gave Abraham Hagar to give her a child. Sarah reacted out of her emotions and made the wrong choice.

How many of us try to handle our situations like Sarah? We make decisions from our emotions, which results in more problems and not solutions. However, we will see that Hannah had emotional moments but she handled them differently.

Her emotions lead her to God whereas Sarah's led her to respond and try to fix it herself. Hannah is a woman that wants to have a child and year after year she waits for this thing to happen for her, yet it has not happened yet.

You and I have had some dreams that we prayed for but as of yet have not happened, so we wait. Sometimes we are able to wait and trust and at other times we become impatient. The true test is, do we allow our emotions to decide on what to do or do we continue to trust in God and wait for His timing? The right answer is we must learn to wait on God's timing for what it is we are seeking.

The Scripture says that God closed her womb. How many of us are waiting for something but it is God who has held up the answer? How do we handle that? Hannah will show us what is necessary. The truth is God already knows the appointed time of our answers for when He will grant what we are waiting for. Let us not become impatient and try to solve things ourselves and make a mess of it. When we try to do things from our emotions the sure result will be more upset than we expected. Sarah was expecting relief but what she received was more rejection when Hagar despised her. As we continue to read about Hannah, we will see how she handles her situation. But the first lesson we can apply is we shouldn't seek to fix our situations from our emotional places because we can surely make the wrong choices.

A Walk With Hannah – How Can I Handle My Bitterness?

> And her adversary also provoked her sore, for to make her fret, because the LORD had shut up her womb. And as he did so year by year, when she went up to the house of the LORD, so she provoked her; therefore she wept, and did not eat. Then said Elkanah her husband to her, Hannah, why weepest thou? and why eatest thou not? and why is thy heart grieved? am not I better to thee than ten sons? So Hannah rose up after they had eaten in Shiloh, and after they had drunk. Now Eli the priest sat upon a seat by a post of the temple of the LORD. And she was in bitterness of soul, and prayed unto the LORD, and wept sore. And she vowed a vow, and said O LORD of hosts, if thou wilt indeed look on the affliction of thine handmaid, and remember me, and not forget thine handmaid, but wilt give unto thine handmaid a man child, then I will give him unto the LORD all the days of his life, and there shall no razor come upon his head. – **1 Samuel 1:6-11 KJV**

We saw in the previous Scripture that Hannah was grieving because she couldn't have any children. To make this situation even worse, Peninnah made herself a yoke around Hannah's neck. She made it her responsibility to remind her of what she could not do. Isn't that like the enemy, to make sure you are reminded daily of your shortcomings and downfalls, such that you begin to fret about what things are not going your way? However, look at the difference between Sarah and Hannah [read Genesis 16 for Sarah's story]. Sarah became so angry that she treated Hagar badly, but Hannah though she became discouraged took her grievances to the Lord.

    Hannah went before the Lord and prayed that God would open up her womb. She even told God that if He would give her this child, that she would dedicate him back to Him. Have you ever made one of those prayers where you ask God to give you something and you promise Him something if He does it? Yet, how many of us really keep that promise once we receive what we have asked for? We will see as we go further that Hannah does keep her promise to the Lord.

    Hannah wanted a child so much that she had become bitter. But she took her bitterness to God and asked Him to handle it. I don't know about you, but I do know I have had some times in my life where I was bitter at the waiting. I got tired of the torment of the devil. And when I couldn't handle it anymore, I had to make it a matter of prayer. The child God was going to birth through Hannah had to come by way of prayer. Sometimes what we are waiting for is waiting on us to pray.

    Hannah's dedication to prayer is the making of a parent's heart. Hannah wanted to be a mother but even as much as she wanted to be one, she wanted most to be an obedient daughter. Before we can be the right kind of parent, we have to first be the right kind of child, a child of God. Hannah waited long to receive the blessings of parenthood, but when it came, she took seriously the role she was given as a parent. Some of us may not have children of our own, but have you been seeking the Lord for "spiritual children"? Have you been asking Him to give you someone you can nurture and encourage? Someone you can guide and teach? When He gives it to you, make sure you keep your promise and have a parent's heart towards them. Do not forsake your duty of leading someone else in the way in which they should go.

      God doesn't give us everything we want, simply because we ask. Sometimes He teaches us patience by making us wait for our prayers to be answered. It is not because He is withholding His goodness from us, but because He is more concerned about our holiness than our immediate earthly happiness. A parent is one that wants what is best for their child, not simply what the child feels is best. So let us take on the true heart of a parent. Let us pass to our natural and spiritual children those things that are best for them, the things of God. Let us also teach them so that they will be equipped in this world to face the realities of life. Let us not give them falsehoods, that life is always happy and filled with drink and merriment. If we do that, we create children that are weak and unable to face the true call for discipleship and sacrifice of this Christian life. Instead, let us show them a true parent's heart and prepare them to face all life's difficulties and circumstances. Life is not always happy, but our lives can have the joy of the Lord so that no matter what we face, we are able to rejoice because we know who we belong to.

A Walk With Hannah – Turn to the One With the Answer

And Eli said unto her, How long wilt thou be drunken? put away thy wine from thee. And Hannah answered and said, No my lord, I am a woman of a sorrowful spirit: I have drunk neither wine nor strong drink, but have poured out my soul before the LORD. Count not thine handmaid for a daughter of Belial: for out of the abundance of my complaint and grief have I spoken hitherto. Then Eli answered and said, Go in peace: and the God of Israel grant thee thy petition that thou hast asked him…Wherefore it came to pass, when the time was come about after Hannah had conceived, that she bare a son, and called his name Samuel, saying, Because I have asked him of the LORD. – **1 Samuel 1:14-17, 20 KJV**

Hannah, even though she had been bitter, did not allow her bitterness to stop her from going to God for help. She was praying so intently that the priest thought she was drunk. She told him no, I have not been drinking but I have come to ask God from the bitterness of my soul to grant me my petition. The best place to take our bitterness is to God. He can handle it and is more than able to help us heal from it.

Hannah asks for a child and tells God she will return the child back to Him. It was not until she released the dream to God that He granted it. So here we have Hannah ready to release the dream she has asked for over and over again into the hand of God. And as we read the Scripture it says, God granted her what she asked.

One of the most important things we learn in our walk is how to trust. As we learn to put our complete trust in God, this helps to develop us into godly parents that then can teach our children how to trust in God in any situation and circumstances. We can do that because we first learned how to do it ourselves. We can teach them who to turn to when they stand in need of answers to life's questions.

We can teach them when life becomes bitter, don't turn to your own understanding or your own devices, but turn to the one that can remove the bitterness from your soul, God. Hannah's dream became more than what she even thought could happen. She wanted a child and God birthed a prophet from her. God's plan for Hannah was always on His heart, she had to align herself with it. For us today, we must remember God's plan is already awaiting us. We must align ourselves in prayer to that plan even when it doesn't appear to be coming. We can't let the devil taunt us into stopping.

Hannah stopped eating. For us, that can look like us stop feeding ourselves spiritually. Don't become malnourished in the Spirit. Keep trusting and praying and then we must give back to God what He provided for us.

A Walk With Hannah – Releasing the Dream

> And when she had weaned him, she took him up with her, with three bullocks, and one ephah of flour, and a bottle of wine, and brought him unto the house of the LORD in Shiloh: and the child was young. And they slew a bullock, and brought the child to Eli. And she said, O my lord, as thy soul liveth, my lord, I am the woman that stood by thee here, praying unto the LORD. For this child I prayed; and the LORD hath given me my petition which I asked of him: therefore also I have lent him to the LORD; as long as he liveth he shall be lent to the LORD. And he worshipped the LORD there. – **1 Samuel 1:24-28 KJV**

God granted Hannah her dream of a son. When Samuel was old enough, Hannah took him to the priest, Eli. She tells Eli here is the "dream" God gave me, I now give it back to Him to use as He decides.

Dreams are a funny thing. We have them and we want them to come true in our way and in our time. Hannah teaches us something about a parent's heart as well as the heart of God. Hannah, who had been sick with despair because she could not have her son, was now ready to release this dream that finally came true. Hannah was able to release Samuel because she realized a vital point and that is, dreams are not for you only. Dreams, while they bring joy to your life, are really to benefit others. Hannah had the pleasure of carrying this dream within her body and the pleasure of bringing this dream to completion. Now the dream was ready to be shared with others. So where do you go with dreams that God has given you? You go back to God. She says as long as he lives, he will be lent (for God's use) to God. Samuel would now become a dream fulfilled that would also affect the lives of others.

What does this show us about parents? As a parent we must bring our children into this world with the mindset that we are going to receive the pleasure of them for a season, but we must release these beautiful dreams back into the hand of the dream giver, God. God wants our children placed in His hand so that He can create in them what is necessary for them to affect the lives of others. God as the ultimate Father wants to create something wonderful inside of us. He wants us to do what Hannah did, come to worship Him. When we do, He can plant in us a dream that He is ready to release into the world. God can take us from places of bitterness in our souls and give us dreams that He will nourish and perfect.

A Walk With Hannah – A Coat Maker

> But Samuel ministered before the LORD, being a child, girded with a linen ephod. Moreover his mother made him a little coat, and brought it to him from year to year, when she came up with her husband to offer the yearly sacrifice. – **1 Samuel 2:18-19 KJV**

Hannah is a nurturing woman. Hannah went from a woman who was hopeless, to a woman with a dream. She released her dream back into the hands of a capable God. Even though God was now the one taking care of the dream, Hannah still had a vital role in the care of this dream. She was the coat maker. Every year her son needed a new coat because he was growing, so she would bring it to him.

Samuel couldn't use the same coat from the year before, because he was growing older, he was growing in stature. His mother used discernment to understand that her son needed to have a coat that would provide him with protection and provisions from the elements. Was this an overcoat like you and I think or was it a regular garment? Whatever it was, it was something he needed to protect him from the elements and to keep him from being exposed.

As a parent (spiritual and natural) it is our responsibility to provide coats to those in our charge. We provide them with the covering they need to keep them from being exposed to things that would destroy them. We provide a coat to keep them protected. We can't give them one coat and think our job is over.

As we grow in spiritual stature we need a new "coat". The old coat will not be enough for the new things we will face. As a parent we have to have discernment to know that our children need a new and bigger coat. They need a bigger coat because the challenges become greater as they grow and they need the armor that will cover them.

Life Lessons

I want to say to all the coat makers in my life, thank you. God can use you to be a coat maker in someone's life that you don't even know. As I wrote the last pages of another book, God was showing me that my words would help someone to be covered, my words would become a "coat" to help them along the way. That's what a coat maker does. Hannah provided her son with the updated covering he needed to function.

What that looks like today is we are willing to provide both the natural "coats" and the spiritual ones. The natural coats are what we willingly provide our children to help them as they grow. As a parent I made sure my children ate, and had clothing. We must be willing to invest in the lives of our children, that's necessary for the heart of a parent.

We must also be willing to invest spiritually. That means we pray, encourage, and teach our children. As they grow, we update how we pray, how we encourage and how we teach. We use discernment like Hannah to know when our children need updated support from us.

A parent's heart must be developed to care for, nurture, and even return our children back to God's use. We let them go because we realize they aren't only for us, but for God's purpose to the world. That baby boy, or little girl you are holding right now has gifts that God wants to use. Raise up that prophet, that evangelist, that apostle and let him or her go to God for His purpose. When we do, that's the best thing a parent's heart can do.

THE INCREASE

JESUS gave us many lessons from His walk on earth. The Scripture Luke 2:52 states, "And Jesus increased in wisdom and stature, and in favour with God and man." Jesus came to save us but also to teach us how to increase in wisdom and spiritual stature before God. He took the time to equip His disciples to be ready to build God's kingdom. These are the same lessons for Christ's disciples today.

Jesus had to do the will of the Father even in the midst of doubt, fear, attack and those who wanted to shut Him up. He knew every encounter had purpose, even the one with Judas. Think about that for a moment. Our Judas encounters have purpose. Judas set in motion God's plan for Jesus' crucifixion. Jesus fulfilled His mission to equip those coming behind to have the tools to finish theirs. The key is we must apply the lessons we learn from Jesus and His walk.

A Walk with Jesus – Wisdom in the Walk

> And there were also with him other little ships. And there arose a great storm of wind, and the waves beat into the ship, so that it was now full. And he was in the hinder part of the ship, asleep on a pillow: and they awake him, and say unto him, Master, carest thou not that we perish? And he arose, and rebuked the wind, and said unto the sea,

Peace be still, And the wind ceased, and there was a great calm. And he said unto them, Why are ye so fearful? How is it that ye have no faith? – **Mark 4:36-40 KJV**

The disciples who walked with Jesus and experienced first-hand His power were afraid when the storm unexpectedly appeared. In that moment the storm became bigger than all that they knew about Jesus and they were afraid. Before we begin to beat them up, we do the same. We have seen Jesus show up again and again in our life and yet, when another storm comes, we do the same thing as the disciples did, we become fearful.

That is why we must remember these words of the Scripture I shared earlier, Luke 2:52. The Scripture stated how Jesus grew and increased in wisdom. Wisdom is us having an understanding of God and how He works, and then applying it to our lives. Jesus increased as He grew. This is what God will do to us as we go through our storms. He will increase our understanding of Him and how He works. As we grow spiritually, so should our wisdom of His ability to keep us through the storms we face.

As we follow God through our storms, we can obtain a good understanding of His ways that will keep us from becoming fearful when the storms arise. Then we will not have to hear Jesus say to us, "How is it that you have little faith?" The Scripture, Psalms 111:10, states, "The fear of the LORD is the beginning of wisdom: a good understanding have all they that do his commandments: his praise endureth for ever." I believe Jesus asked His disciples about their faith because He had been with them and they should have realized His power.

Again, I don't want to be hard on the disciples because we do the same things. But this is our admonishment to begin to seek wisdom to understand God's ways and how He will show up in our situations. The disciples had Jesus on the boat with them. He was sleeping, at rest; but they were not. How many times are we restless about the things we are experiencing and we want the Lord to appear more concerned than He seems to be? But instead of them questioning Jesus' concern for them, they should have realized if He was resting, they should have found rest as well.

We must take our journey with God through our seasons of storms, with a reverence for Him so that we can obtain wisdom and understanding of His ways. That way when we leave one storm and another one unexpectedly comes, we won't be afraid. We can remember who speaks to our storms to calm them. Additionally, we must remember that He will keep us through the storms, until He is ready to speak, peace be still.

A Walk With Jesus – Lifts the Burdens
> Cast thy burden upon the LORD, and he shall sustain thee: he shall never suffer the righteous to be moved. –
> **Psalm 55:22 KJV**

Going back to the previous Scripture, Mark 4:36-40, we were told a storm came upon the disciples. Now remember these men were fishermen so they were aware of the unexpected storms that would come upon the sea. But there was something about this storm that had them afraid. Maybe it was a storm stronger than any they had ever experienced. Whatever it was, this storm didn't just hit the ship that Jesus was in with the disciples but the Scripture says there were smaller ships with them that were affected as well. The water was coming strong and the boat was now filling up with the waters.

We can have sympathy on how they might feel. You're in your own storm that came upon you unexpectedly. Not just you alone, but the storm is also affecting those that are counting on you or are waiting for you to lead them. You are caught unawares and now the storm is coming at you full force, and it looks like it is going to pull you under, what are you to do?

We can understand why the disciples were afraid. Yet, how should we handle this? It doesn't matter the type of storm, because any of them God is ready for. Maybe today your storm is a financial one. You've lost your job and the "little" ships are depending on you to lead them, but you feel like the storm is taking you under. Maybe it's physical and you're sick and you're wondering, how am I going to take care of these "ships" depending on me to see them to the other side? Maybe it's within your relationship, husband or wife gone and now it all falls to you, how will you take care of these little ships?

In the midst of this storm God is going to increase your ability to stand. It doesn't matter that the water seems to be coming up over the side of the boat, because if need be, Jesus can call you to come and walk on top of the water to see you to the other side.

What is the key to our success? It is keeping our focus on the master. God gives us a great promise in the Scripture above. He tells us to give Him whatever burdens us. Whatever has us heavy and unable to see our way clear. Whatever has us doubting, or fearful, we are to bring it to Him. And God's promise is He will sustain us.

Jesus shows us this promise when He calms the storm for the disciples. He calms the storm not only for the big ship but He also calms the storm for the "little ships". Know today that God will not only calm our storms and keep us safe, but He will calm it for those with us. He will continue to give us what we need so that the "little ships" with us can also make it through.

A Walk With Jesus - Secure in His Promises

> Teaching them to observe all things whatsoever I have commanded you: and, lo, I am with you always, even unto the end of the world. Amen. – **Matthew 28:20 KJV**

Continuing with the previous Scripture, the storm is overtaking them, they don't see Jesus so they go in search of Him. When they find Him, He is asleep. How can He be sleeping at a time like this is probably what they are thinking? They ask Jesus a question, why don't you care about us, why are you asleep?

You know that feeling. You are in the midst of a storm that is getting worse and you don't see God, so you ask, "don't you love me?" "Why aren't You coming to rescue me?" Martha and Mary had the same talk with Jesus. "If you had been here, my brother would not have died" (John 11:21). We don't understand why the storms rage; they don't make sense to us.

Why should I have money problems when I go to work every day and take care of my family? Why does there always seem to be one thing after the other going wrong? Why should I have problems with my kids when I am a good Christian doing as I should? So we go to God and ask, why don't You care about me? In the midst of our storm, God wants to increase our understanding and wisdom about His ways regarding the storms we face. He keeps the storms from destroying us. And He doesn't leave us alone to face them. He is there all the way through.

Jesus was asleep but the disciples forgot an important fact– Jesus was on the boat! He wasn't on the shore looking at them. He was right there in the midst of the storm on the ship. That is where we need Jesus, right in the midst of our hearts when the storms begin to rage so that we can rest in the assurance of His words. The Scripture above is a reminder that Jesus will never leave us. He promises to be with us until the end of the world. He isn't unaware or caught off guard by our storms. He knows the storms are coming even before we do.

We need to allow God to increase our assurance in His power. He is going to be with us through every storm, every wind and every rain that comes. He does care for us and that is why He gives us the promise that He will be with us until the end. It is our responsibility to Trust Him!

A Walk With Jesus – Rest in Jesus

> Rest in the LORD, and wait patiently for him: fret not thyself because of him who prospereth in his way, because the man who bringeth wicked devices to pass. – **Psalm 27:7 KJV**

When the disciples went frantically looking for Jesus, they found Him sleeping. How could it be that Jesus was sleeping in the midst of a storm? I believe Jesus was trying to teach a great message not only to the disciples then, but also to us now. The disciples thought Jesus unaware because He was asleep. Jesus was fully aware of the storm; He just chooses to rest through it.

How could He rest through a storm? I mean the winds are blowing, the waves are tossing the boat and the water is coming in and filling the boat full? Jesus chooses to rest because He is not afraid of the storm, Jesus knows His Father will take care of Him because He has not yet finished the Father's plan.

We can rest in God because He is our Father and He is not allowing the storm to come and destroy us, no matter what it looks like to the natural eye. The spiritual eye sees differently. It is in these storms that God wants to increase our awareness of His strength. He says come while the storm rages and you'll find rest, peace and joy in Me. How could someone understand how you have been given a diagnosis of illness but yet you are rejoicing? That is because you are resting [trusting God to carry you].

The psalmist tells us to rest in the Lord. In our time of resting we wait for God and do not worry about those who the enemy uses against us. We don't worry because we know in God's time He will make the attack stop and the storm will cease. And what has happened? You have been increased, step-by-step through your process. You have gained wisdom through your storm about how God cares for you.

God's people are increased in godly power as they stand in the midst of their storms and allow the work of the master to be done. We must learn to rest in Jesus. We must know that we can lay our heads down and rest at night even if we don't know where the next check is coming from. Why because our Father has all provisions and He will take care of us. Maybe, just maybe God is allowing those times of lack to help us learn that He is our provider and sustainer. It is not our job, but our God.

> O LORD, how manifold are thy works! in wisdom hast thou made them all: the earth is full of thy riches. So is this great and wide sea, wherein are things creeping innumerable, both small and great beast. – **Psalm 104:24-25 KJV**

So Jesus calms the storm and then asks them, why are you so fearful, where is your faith? On the other end of the storm, yes we can say we trust you Jesus. But in the midst of the storm sometimes we became fearful. The disciples aren't much different than us. We have great praise reports *after* the storms, but not so much in the midst of the storms. However, what is it that God wants to increase in us in the midst of our storms?

He wants to increase our trust in Him. That is why He tells us to reverence Him and get an understanding of His ways. In doing so, we will prosper in all our ways. He wants to increase us in wisdom for our "storm" walks. He also wants us to trust completely in Him to give Him all our burdens. He wants to increase our assurance in His abilities to calm the storms in our lives in His time and in His way. And as He does this, we can surely rest in Him.

He wants us to learn in the midst of the storm to praise Him. The psalmist thanks God for His creation of the seas, and these are the same seas that the disciples are now fighting as the storms rage upon it. Why praise Him for the seas that rage? Well if He can make the seas, surely

He can calm the storm on it? While God may not be the cause of the storms in our lives, He gives the permission for them to come. Therefore those same storms that needed the permission to come must obey the voice of the One who granted it.

The storm ends. The boat no longer is tossed by the winds and rain. The smaller ships are also at peace. And what is greatest is this, all the ships have experienced a greater understanding of what it is that Jesus can do. They all have received an increase!

If you are in the midst of a storm, ask God to fill you with His presence and increase His good gifts within you. Ask Him to fill your cup and run it over so that you have an abundance of what you need. If you are coming out of a storm, thank Him for the storm, because He used it to show Himself mighty. And if you are on the verge of a storm coming, do not fear, remind yourself who can calm the storm and who is on the water with you. Jesus is in you and greater is He that is in you than He that is in the world. Go praising God for all His blessings to you. The storms end.

Life Lessons

Jesus consistently used every moment to teach His disciples the truth about Him and the Father. The storm they faced was another opportunity for Jesus to teach the disciples how to walk like Him. He had assurance that the Father would answer His request. Why? First, because Jesus already knew what His assignment was and it had not yet transpired. While we don't know the time and hour we will be called home to be with Jesus, we can still walk in confidence that God listens to us. God allows the storms in our lives to help us grow in our confidence in Him.

If we seek Him to calm the storms we face, we must have faith that He will. The second lesson Jesus teaches us is–Don't become panicked by what we see. Yes, this wasn't just a slight storm, but it was enough to tear the boat apart. Yet, Jesus slept. We are admonished to find our rest in God because of what Jesus offers us. Jesus has given each of us the right to approach God and have expectation and the belief that we will see a miracle. We must believe for it! God used the storms to increase our trust through showing Himself faithful.

And finally, we want to be able to answer Jesus' question of where is your faith, with a resounding, "I am walking in it because I trusted You". We want to rest in God's promises because the storm will end. On the other side of them, God has increased us in trust, faith, and ability.

UNUSUAL ASSIGNMENTS

JEHOSHAPHAT was 35 when he became king, and he reigned for 25 years (2 Chronicles 20:31). While Jehoshaphat showed a high regard for justice in his dealings (2 Chronicles 19:4-11) he didn't make a wise choice when dealing with Ahab. Jehoshaphat, as well as his father, Asa, did bring good to counteract the idolatry of the time. Both had their weaknesses, but it was their faith in God that helped them during their reign. Jehoshaphat shows us the importance of accepting unusual assignments from God.

David, Abraham, Sarah and Job also show us what happens in the lives of everyday people who encounter God's assignment for the unusual. The question is what will we do with that assignment? Will we follow the leading of God's Spirit and obey, or will we turn away because it appears too hard? What did these individuals do when faced with their unusual assignments?

A Walk with Jehosphaphat – Men on the Frontline

> [21]After consulting the people, the king appointed singers to walk ahead of the army, singing to the Lord and praising him for his holy splendor. This is what they sang: "Give thanks to the Lord; his faithful love endures forever!" [22]At the very moment they began to sing and

give praise, the Lord caused the armies of Ammon, Moab, and Mount Seir to start fighting among themselves. – **2 Chronicles 20:21-22 NLT**

I heard a powerful message some time ago based on this Scripture. When this Scripture was read the Lord asked me a question. He asked, what if the singers had refused to take their assignment? They could have said, "Who me?" Why don't you send the men with the arrows and weapons ahead? Or better yet, God why don't You go out ahead of us, because I'm not sure this plan will work. God then spoke to me and said, "Do not run from unusual assignments."

What is an *unusual assignment*? That is anything that is not what you would expect, anything that requires you to do the unexpected. In other words, that means you have to give up your expectations, your agenda, your way of thinking and be willing to be used as God says. I have an example of this type of assignment. I remember when God told me to bend down and speak to the womb of a young lady wanting to get pregnant. He told me to tell the womb to bring forth a child. Well that young lady is very soon going to deliver that child. But what if I had refused the unusual assignment?

Unusual assignments. God is calling for some people to step to the front line and be used by God His way. It calls for us to strip off our own weapons or ideas of how to fight, and take on God's plan of warfare. God told these men to sing and praise Him. If you see what happens, when they begin to sing (walk in obedience), the other armies are confused by the singing and they kill each other. This unusual assignment brought about great victory. It is in the unusual things that God can bring great victory in our lives and the lives of others. God calls for obedient men and women to take their post.

Jehoshaphat appointed singers. God does the same, He has called us to an appointment of salvation and when we hear and obey, He places us in His family. Then when we allow Him to develop us, He sends us to the mission. God enacted the mission, Jesus fulfilled the mission, the Holy Spirit enabled us for the mission, and we are to carry the mission to the world.

We should not be afraid of the unusual assignments in our lives. Let us do as these men did, they accepted their mission and willingly went before the enemy with praise and singing. This is what the Lord called War-ship, when praise becomes our weapons. So, let's use this weapon in our situations and see the salvation of the LORD!

A Walk With David – Small Things Can Win Battles

> [45] David replied to the Philistine, "You come to me with sword, spear, and javelin, but I come to you in the name of the Lord of Heaven's Armies—the God of the armies of Israel, whom you have defied. [48] As Goliath moved closer to attack, David quickly ran out to meet him. [49] Reaching into his shepherd's bag and taking out a stone, he hurled it with his sling and hit the Philistine in the forehead. The stone sank in, and Goliath stumbled and

fell face down on the ground. ⁵⁰ So David triumphed over the Philistine with only a sling and a stone, for he had no sword. – **1 Samuel 17:45, 48-50 NLT**

We have probably read or heard many messages about David and Goliath. David was a young boy that was not afraid of the giant standing before him. The army would go to the battle, but when the giant would come and challenge them, they would run. That is how we are at times. We go to church and get in our positions but as soon as big situations come, we run and hide because we don't think we can overcome them.

David knew that God was bigger than this giant and he was ready to take this unusual assignment. It was unusual because who would send a boy to do a warrior's job? Who would, God would. God will send us into situations that sometimes others say we are not ready to handle. But God does differently, because He can use our small weapons to defeat the enemy. He can use them, because we trust Him instead of running from the battle. That is what David did. He ran quickly to the battle line with only a sling and a few rocks. *Unusual weapons*. But then we serve an unusual God that can do unusual things.

If we give even our smallest of gifts and talents to God, He will use them to advance the battle for others. The army would not have gone forward, until someone stepped up and took care of Goliath. God used David to rally others to battle. He took the unexpected warrior David, and won the battle. God will take us, the unexpected warriors, and win battles for us and others.

David didn't discount his size; don't let others discount yours, even yourself. There are times when we can think we do not have enough for God to use. However, He is only seeking us to be willing. When we are, He will do the rest. So I pray that we would quickly run to our post in the Lord's army. And when we do, God will take our all and use it to win the battles.

A Walk With Abraham – Unshakable Faith

> Some time later, God tested Abraham's faith. "Abraham!" God called. "Yes," he replied. "Here I am." [2] "Take your son, your only son—yes, Isaac, whom you love so much—and go to the land of Moriah. Go and sacrifice him as a burnt offering on one of the mountains, which I will show you." [3] The next morning Abraham got up early. He saddled his donkey and took two of his servants with him, along with his son, Isaac. Then he chopped wood for a fire for a burnt offering and set out for the place God had told him about. [5] "Stay here with the donkey," Abraham told the servants. "The boy and I will travel a little farther. We will worship there, and then we will come right back." – **Genesis 22:1-3, 5 NLT**

Abraham was a man of great faith in God. We see this evident in these verses. Abraham received a promise from God for an heir. After many years of waiting for the promise, it finally came to pass. Can you imagine how it feels to have a promise of God finally realized? It had to be a wonderful thing to see the evidence of God's promise fulfilled in his life.

Now, after having that promise fulfilled, God tells Abraham to take the son that you love and offer him to Me as a burnt offering. There was no confusing this command. God was telling Abraham to kill his son; the son God had given him. Abraham could have doubted God and even become angry because of the request being made to give up something he had just waited so long to receive; yet Scripture shows otherwise.

Abraham rose up early to be obedient to God. He didn't wait, he didn't try to change the command, and he rose early to accomplish what he was told to do. He took some young men and told them, you stay here while the lad and I go to worship and we will come back. Such faith!! Those few words spoke much about Abraham. He knew he was going to kill his son, but he also knew that this same son was promised and through him would come many nations, so how did he reconcile the two? The Scripture does not tell us, but this we can glean, he knew that the God he served would fulfill His promise. Maybe God would raise him again, might have been the thought Abraham had. Whatever it was, he was trusting in God. So he said we will go to worship and *we will return.*

This encourages us that we must be willing to trust God with unshakable faith. He is calling all believers to this unusual assignment. God is calling us to let go of everything, all that we love into His hands. This can be difficult to do, because we know that these may be things that God has promised us and we see our future in them. Yet, God is saying, go and sacrifice it on a high mountain (laying it on the altar before Him). And our response to God when He calls us to sacrifice everything before Him must be yes.

We should rise early to the task and go to worship Him and trust that even in the midst of our sacrificing we will return with all God's promises still available to us. That is the message in these Scriptures, that even when God calls us to prove our trust in Him we can go to the unusual assignment and return with all God's promises in our lives as a yes. God does not lie, therefore what He promises, He will fulfill.

We must rise up quickly and go to our unusual assignments of being people with unshakable faith in God. When we do this, we can know that not only will God keep His promise, but He will also reward us for being obedient to the things He calls us to do; those things that really don't make sense to us.

A Walk With Sarah - *No laughing Matter*

> [9] "Where is Sarah, your wife?" the visitors asked. "She's inside the tent," Abraham replied. [10] Then one of them said, "I will return to you about this time next year, and your wife, Sarah, will have a son!" Sarah was listening to this conversation from the tent. [11] Abraham and Sarah were both very old by this time, and Sarah was long past the age of having children. [12] So she laughed silently to herself and said, "How could a worn-out woman like me enjoy such pleasure, especially when my master—my husband—is also so old?" [13] Then the Lord said to Abraham, "Why did Sarah laugh? Why did she say, 'Can an old woman like me have a baby?' [14] Is anything too hard for the Lord? I will return about this time next year, and Sarah will have a son."... [1] The Lord kept his word and did for Sarah exactly what he had promised. [2] She became pregnant, and she gave birth to a son for Abraham in his old age. This happened at just the time God had said it would. – **Genesis 18:9-14, 21:1-2 NLT**

When we read Scripture, we often look at the main character and sometimes forget about the lessons that can be learned from the supporting cast of characters. We know about Abraham and his great faith, but what about his wife, what can we learn from Sarah's life? God made a promise to Abraham that he would give him an heir, yet these were conversations between Abraham and God, we do not see Sarah in the conversations.

However, in this meeting, Sarah overhears the conversation. Abraham is told he will have a son with Sarah and that the Lord would visit at his appointed time when this was to happen. Sarah hears and she laughs. She laughs because she knows the "physical" truth. That is, her body has passed the childbearing age and she has let go of this dream.

Have some of you let go of some dreams because you think it is past its time to be born in you? Do you laugh because you think that boat has sailed and there's no way you can do that thing? Let us listen to God's answer to Sarah's laughing. He says, is there anything too hard for God?

Have you ever wondered, "Why did God wait so long to allow Abraham and Sarah to have a child?" It could be that God wanted to show Himself capable of doing the impossible. For what is impossible with man, is not with God. Had they been able to have a child, they may not have associated it with God's doing, but something they were able to do within their own capacities. This was a surety that God did it. And God, who is faithful, came at the appointed time and worked within Sarah's body for her to conceive and bring forth a child. The things in her body that had ceased, He renewed. That which had died, He brought back to life, so that His plan could be fulfilled. God can bring life into a womb void of life, and He can place life in a womb without the help of man's intervention (as He did with Mary).

God is calling some of us to unusual assignments, bringing spiritual life from within our beings when we may think it is too late. Nothing is too hard for God. May God show us what promise He wants to fulfill within our lives. And when He does, don't laugh. This is no laughing matter, for God will do as He says. At the appointed time, He will come and fulfill His promise. Allow Him access today to bring the promise forth from the unusual assignment He has given to you. And instead of laughing at it being impossible, rejoice at it being done!

A Walk With Job – Right Attitude Through Suffering

> [9] His wife said to him, "Are you still trying to maintain your integrity? Curse God and die."[10] But Job replied, "You talk like a foolish woman. Should we accept only good things from the hand of God and never anything bad?" So in all this, Job said nothing wrong…[12] So the Lord blessed Job in the second half of his life even more than in the beginning. For now he had 14,000 sheep, 6,000 camels, 1,000 teams of oxen, and 1,000 female donkeys. [13] He also gave Job seven more sons and three more daughters. – **Job 2:9-10; 42:12-13 NLT**

In the last chapter, we talked about the supporting characters within a story line. We have heard about Job, but what about his wife? Most of the time when we read this small piece of Scripture we tend to say shame on her. We however forget something very important. Those children that were killed were also her children. The property and things that were lost were also hers.

Now she had to watch her husband wasting away, and she was being pushed to the limits in her grief, because she could not understand why God was allowing this to happen to her husband. So she becomes angry with Job and asks, "Are you still trying to say you have integrity, if so, why is God doing this to you?" When we look at it from that point of view, we understand that this was not an easy assignment for either of them. Grief can become an unusual assignment to handle. Now, let me say this, Job's wife didn't handle it well. She was tired of going through and she just wanted it to be over. How many of us can understand that? We go through our situations and circumstances and we want to simply say, **"God take this away!"**

Job answered her and said you are speaking foolishly. Can we expect to receive blessing from God but not evil? What Job is really saying is we cannot expect everything to always be good. Some difficulties will come into our lives and we must not become foolish in how we handle them. God calls us to handle our unusual assignments through times of grief, trusting in Him and keeping ourselves from sin. Yet, I want to show you something really important. God extends forgiveness to this grieving wife and mother. How do I know that? It says that in Job's latter days he was blessed with plenty and he also had more children. It does not say anything about him getting another wife, so we can surmise that it was with this same wife.

Today, I pray that we understand at times we will go through some difficult situations with those that we love and we may not always understand the "why". Let us not do as Job's wife did and allow our grief to get the best of us. We must remember that in the good times God is there, as well as during our difficulties. And we can stand on this promise that God will never leave us in our difficulties.

If God has an unusual assignment for you, don't run from it because it is through these unusual assignments that God shows himself great. Sometimes unusual assignments call for us to let go completely of ourselves and those things we are comfortable with. *Let them go!* Sometimes unusual assignments call for us to let go of preconceived ideas and notions on how things will work. *Let them go!* Unusual assignments call for us to step out of our comfort zones and to walk by faith and not by sight. They also call us to let go of the fear of what things look like. *Let them go!* When we do, God promises to bring something wonderful from our lives because of our obedience to Him in those unusual situations.

Life Lessons

God is looking for a people willing to accept unusual assignments. These are the assignments where great victories are won against situations that look like sure defeat. He is looking for a David to step in and face a giant. God is looking for a people who will worship their way through some battles that appear to have us closed in.

God is looking for some people who have come to the end of hope and believe it is too late for their dream to be fulfilled; because He will do the unexpected. And like Sarah we may want to laugh about it because of the disbelief, but faith will bring us to the place of realizing it.

God is looking for some sons and daughters who have suffered much but won't curse Him. Those who will live and see the goodness of the Lord. Like Jehoshaphat we can see the enemy destroyed even while we praise. God's people took the challenge to walk in the unusual assignments that allowed God to perform miracles. When we take the challenge for the unusual, we can expect God to bring forth unusual manifestations!

FIRST THINGS FIRST

MARY AND MARTHA are the sisters of Lazarus. We don't know a lot about their family background. It is believed that Martha is the oldest because the house is referred to as Martha's.[1] What is known is they loved each other deeply. We also know of the event where Jesus came to their house and Martha was upset that Mary wasn't helping her with the chores for the guest.

Mary decided to sit at Jesus' feet and let Him serve her, while Martha was focused on serving Him. How often do we become like Martha? We are so focused on serving Him that we forget to allow Him to serve us. Through our walk with Mary and Martha we will be reminded on how to put the right things in the right place.

A Walk With Mary and Martha –Martha Why Are You Worried?

> "Now it happened as they went that He entered a certain village; and a certain woman named Martha welcomed Him into her house. And she had a sister called Mary, who also sat at Jesus' feet and heard His word. But Martha was distracted with much serving, and she approached Him and said, 'Lord, do You not care that my sister has left me to serve alone? Therefore tell her to help

---

[1] Youngblood, R.F. Editor. *Nelson New Illustrated Bible Dictionary*. "Mary." p. 807.

me. And Jesus answered and said to her, 'Martha, Martha, you are worried and troubled about *many things*, But *one thing* is needed, and Mary has chosen that good part, which will not be taken away from her." – **Luke 10:38-42, NKJV, Italics added**

When we read this Scripture we see that Jesus was coming to Martha's house and she was busy trying to have everything *perfect* for serving the Lord. As she was making preparations in her home, her sister Mary was seated at the feet of Jesus, listening and receiving His word.

Martha (like us) became frustrated that she was busy working and it seemed to her that Mary was getting away without helping. So Martha went to Jesus and began to complain about how her sister wasn't helping. Martha wanted to know if Jesus was going to do something about it.

Jesus' response to Martha was, you are worried and troubled about many things but you are missing the one thing that is needed. And He said Mary has chosen it. *What had Mary chosen?* She had chosen to be served by Jesus. She had chosen to come and be filled with the word by sitting at His feet.

Martha's idea to serve Jesus was a good one, but she missed what was necessary for her. We have to be careful not to become distracted with busy work. Sometimes we are told that it is our serving that shows our true relationship to God. That is only partially true. When we love the Lord we will serve Him, but service without a deep personal relationship with the Lord will only lead us to be frustrated, worried, and troubled about many things. We can find ourselves doing the outer work, like Martha did of cleaning the house and preparing the food, but leaving the inner work undone. Mary did the latter.

Mary was seeking the first things first. What is the first thing? It is us seeking to hear from the Lord and to be served by His Spirit. When we do this, we can do the "good" part of what Martha was doing, which is to give our service back to the Lord. Additionally, when we do the first works of getting away with the Lord, we will discover we aren't frustrated about what others are doing because we have been refreshed in God ourselves.

We must seek God's direction for our lives to know which way He wants us to go. We do not want to depend on our serving *alone*. We must be willing to adjust our pace as well as to make time to sit at the Lord's feet and receive from Him. Martha's schedule didn't have Jesus on the agenda. Oh yes, she was ready to serve Him but He wasn't on her agenda to worship with Him. We must make sure that we don't leave time with Jesus out when we plan to serve Him.

A Walk With Mary and Martha –Martha Why Are You Worried? (Part 2)

> "Now it happened as they went that He entered a certain village; and a certain woman named Martha welcomed Him into her house. And she had a sister called Mary,

who also sat at Jesus' feet and heard His word. But Martha was distracted with much serving, and she approached Him and said, 'Lord, do You not care that my sister has left me to serve alone? Therefore tell her to help me. And Jesus answered and said to her, 'Martha, Martha, you are worried and troubled about *many things*, But *one thing* is needed, and Mary has chosen that good part, which will not be taken away from her." – **Luke 10:38-42, NKJV, Italics added**

In the previous chapter we took a look at this Scripture, but there is still so much more that we can glean from these verses. Let's look a little closer at Martha. Martha was busy trying to serve Jesus. She allowed herself to become worried about the preparation she was doing for Jesus' visit. She was so busy that the reason for His coming was lost in the preparation. Martha lost sight of the fact that the *Messiah* was coming to her house. Her focus was more on making sure He was pleased with her work, than on what she could receive from spending time in His presence.

Martha shows us something about ourselves that we need to address. Are we too busy preparing for Jesus to come that we have lost sight of the fact that He has asked us to invite Him into our houses? Not just our physical houses (home, church, etc.), but also into our spiritual houses. Jesus wants to dwell with us. He stands at the door of our hearts and knocks. The most important thing is to allow Him access to our spiritual house. He does not want us to spend all our efforts *worried* about preparing for Him to come. This goes for our churches as well. Jesus does not want us spending our time troubled about many things on how to serve Him, but to allow Him access and then to listen at His feet to His directions.

This reminds me of those that believe they have to *clean house* first, before they can accept Jesus as their Savior. We can never prepare enough before we accept Christ into our lives. We have to invite Him in, and then allow Him to direct us in how to *clean house*. Hint, we cannot do it by ourselves. That's what causes us to become frustrated and worried about many things, we are trusting in our own efforts. Even though they may be good ideas, it is simply not going to work in our own efforts.

We must be willing to release all the service acts we hold in our hand. We need to ask some important questions; Lord is this what You want me to do? Lord am I so busy trying to serve You that I am not taking time to be served by You? And Lord, am I trying so hard to work my way into your presence that I have forgotten that it only comes by trusting in You? There is an order we must remember to keep. We go to God first, to allow Him to clean us, shape us, and make us into the image of His Son. And when we do that we are also being equipped to serve well.

A Walk With Mary and Martha –Mary Chooses the Better Way.

> Then, six days before the Passover, Jesus came to Bethany, where Lazarus was who had been dead, whom He had raised from the dead. ² There they made Him a supper; and Martha served, but Lazarus was one of those who sat at the table with Him. ³ Then Mary took a pound of very costly oil of spikenard, anointed the feet of Jesus, and wiped His feet with her hair. And the house +was filled with the fragrance of the oil. – **John 12:1-3 NKJV**

What about Mary? In the previous Scripture Mary sat at Jesus' feet and listened to His words. She allowed herself to be fed so that she could then serve Jesus. We see in these verses that Mary now gives her service unto Christ. She takes an ointment and anoints Jesus' feet and then she uses her own hair to wipe His feet. The Scripture says the smell of this gift fills the entire house with its fragrance.

These words bring to mind some very important things that we should be incorporating into our lives. Mary put first things first. She came to learn at Jesus' feet. Then she takes the next step to give her service unto Christ. Martha was serving, but what was the difference? Martha was busy with serving for the sake of serving, but Mary was serving with the desire to express her total love for the savior.

Scripture does not mention any words or actions from Mary that express anything other than love. Mary gives what is costly. She is not stingy with her giving. She is not worried if anyone else's gift was as much as hers. Her focus was all on Jesus. That's the difference between Mary's gift and Martha's. Martha was looking around her (that's why she was frustrated that she didn't see her sister working) but Mary was looking at Jesus only.

The reward for being willing to give your all to Jesus is that your gift will be like the sweet smell of the ointment that Mary poured on Jesus. When we allow God to fill us up, then we are able to give back to the service of the Lord. When we give our service to the Lord from a submitted heart it is like Mary pouring the oil. We pour out our service to Him and God uses it to fill the house. Not just our own houses, but God's house, His church. The fragrance of our action lingers and those that are there experience it. Those that were in the house with Mary had the opportunity to experience the fragrance of her gift. Some will appreciate it and others will complain what you do is too costly, but we must simply do what is pleasing to God.

We must go to the Lord first and receive His instruction. Then our desire to be served by God's spirit turns into our ability to serve others. When we go to serve we do it out of our love and not out of a sense of duty. We do not want to be troubled by many things. Yet, we want our love for Christ to be evident in all that we do. Are you willing to sit at Jesus' feet and pour out all for Him?

A Walk With Mary and Martha –Mary and Martha Responses.

⁵ So although Jesus loved Martha, Mary, and Lazarus, ⁶ he stayed where he was for the next two days. – **John 11:5-6 NLT**

I have always found this Scripture interesting. Why? Because it starts by telling us how much Jesus loved Martha and Mary. Yet, it says He stayed where He was for the next two days. He loved them but He didn't move at their initial request. How many times have we called for the Lord to fix something in our lives yet, it appeared He wasn't moved or didn't care because He didn't move at our initial request. Maybe the reason was the same reason why He didn't move for Martha and Mary, there was a greater outcome to be manifested.

A quick recap. Martha was frustrated at Mary for not helping her do the work to prepare for Jesus' coming. And in fact, she had a bit of an attitude with Jesus because He didn't make her help. Mary went and listened and received from Jesus. She made the best choice. But that doesn't mean we always have the right responses or that we fully understand all the lessons as they come. Now we have the two sisters calling for Jesus to come. I can only imagine they thought He would come immediately because they had that kind of relationship with Him. But He didn't come. In fact, in His not coming we learn that Lazarus died.

Before we move to the next part of this story, let's just take a moment of reflection on what we may have felt. Would you have been upset? Jesus, why didn't you stop my loved one from dying? Would you have felt helpless? Jesus, we saw you heal and raise others. We thought You loved us, why did you hesitate in coming?

The lesson we get is that there will be times that even though we know we are loved by God, His answer won't come in the time we think. But we must remember to still trust, and continue to hold on to the truth that His love for us is greater than what our situations look like.

A Walk With Mary and Martha –Mary and Martha's Responses (Part, 2).

> [20] When Martha got word that Jesus was coming, she went to meet him. But Mary stayed in the house. [21] Martha said to Jesus, "Lord, if only you had been here, my brother would not have died. [22] But even now I know that God will give you whatever you ask." – **John 11:20-22 NLT**

Martha and Mary respond to Jesus' delay. When He arrives, Mary stays in the house but Martha goes out to Him. Martha says to Jesus, if You had been here, my brother would not have died. Let's look at that first. First, Martha understood the power in Jesus. She knew He was more than able to stop death. But even in this statement, there is a little bit of frustration.

What do I mean? She is essentially saying you didn't come when we called You. Could that be part of why Mary didn't even come out to Him? The Scripture doesn't say that specifically, but let's be honest about how we deal with our emotional situations. How many of us would have also been upset? You say you love us but You allowed us to suffer this loss. That's what many of us believe about our Christian walk. We believe that we are exempt from some things because Jesus loves us. The understanding we must walk away with is yes, we are loved; but we also face difficulties and hardships.

Martha went on to say, but even now, God will give you what You ask. Martha had the understanding that Jesus could still fix the situation even though it looked hopeless. We must be willing to continue to trust God's processes even when they don't always make sense to us.

I believe in this instance; we too would respond like either Martha or Mary. We might refuse to even go into dialogue with God because we are too overwhelmed by the grief of our loss, or we will come to the meeting but still have some doubt, frustration or concerns. Part of us wants to hold on to the truth, but sometimes we don't. We know the outcome of this story; Jesus does raise Lazarus.

Life Lessons

There are times when we show up to our life situations either in a Martha the worrier way or as a Mary who sits at the feet of Jesus. But there are times when we also show up as Martha that's willing to come to meet with Jesus even when we don't understand His delay to our request. Or we become Mary who is so overwhelmed with our grief that we can't even come to meet with God.

The truth is we need to balance our Martha and Mary tendencies. We need to check that work attitude which causes us to forget to spend time with God and not just do work for God. We need to encourage that Mary part of us that stops and sits at Jesus' feet to learn from Him but to also be equipped to serve Him.

Additionally, we need to encourage the side of us to continue to go to God even when we don't think our situation is working in our favor. We have to continue to build trust. And we need to encourage that other side of us that shuts down and doesn't even have the strength to go seeking and asking in the midst of our difficulties. We all have some Martha and Mary in us, we must learn which parts to nurture and what parts to change. In allowing God to grow us, we continue to put the most important parts first, sitting at His feet to receive from Him.

THE OFFENSE

ADAM is the first man, created by God on the sixth day of creation. God placed him in the garden of Eden (Gen. 2:19-23; :8-9, 17, 20-21; 4:1, 25; 5:1-5). He and his wife Eve, created by God from one of Adam's ribs, became the ancestors to all people now living on earth. God gave Adam instructions to work the land and to be fruitful and multiply.

Genesis 3 tells us how Adam failed to keep the instructions of the Lord. Now, there is much debate about why Adam was blamed for this sin when it was Eve who had the conversation with the serpent. Allow me for a moment to interject (you can agree or disagree). Adam received the instructions from God (Genesis 2). So when Eve had the conversation with the serpent, this is what the Scripture reports in Genesis 3:6 NLT, "The woman was convinced. She saw that the tree was beautiful and its fruit looked delicious, and she wanted the wisdom it would give her. So she took some of the fruit and ate it. Then she gave some to her husband, who was with her, and he ate it, too."

Did you catch that last part, he was with her. He stood and listened to her have this conversation with the serpent and he didn't interject, stop it or protect her from creating this offense. We don't have the conversation that was going on in Adam's mind, so we don't know why he didn't stop her. But this first created man, Adam was the door opener to the great offense.

A Walk With Adam – Man's Purpose

> "And God said, Let us make man in our image, after our likeness: and let them have dominion over the fish of the sea, and over the fowl of the air, and over the cattle, and over all the earth, and over every creeping thing that creepeth upon the earth. So God created man in his own image, in the image of God created he him; male and female created he them. And God blessed them, and God said unto them, Be fruitful, and multiply, and replenish the earth, and subdue it: and have dominion over the fish and of the sea, and over the fowl of the air, and over every living thing that moveth upon the earth…And God saw everything that he had made, and, behold it was very good." – **Genesis 1:26-28, 31a KJV**

In this Scripture, there was a conversation going on with God the Father, God the Son and God the Holy Spirit. It was decided that God would create man in His image. God gave to mankind attributes that were distinctly His, that no other animal possessed (we were not apes).

Humanity has the ability to create and to reason, for example, because these are attributes of God that He shares with us. God also gave man a place of honor when He gave him lordship over the earth. Furthermore, God blessed Adam and Eve and gave them directives to bring forth fruit of their own kind. When God saw what He had done, He said it was very good.

God created man for a purpose. He created man first and foremost to honor Him. God was pleased with what He did in man. He blessed Adam and Eve by giving them access to all that He created. This story that started out as one filled with potential, was changed because of sin. Yet, we can glean so much from this Scripture.

We can understand that God has a purpose for all humanity. When God created us, He had a purpose for us. First and foremost our purpose is to praise and honor God. He also is calling for us to be fruitful and multiply. We tend to look at this Scripture primarily as bringing forth children by birth, but it also carries a spiritual message. We are to spiritually birth children who we bring to God to allow Him to change. We then must walk with them, train them and help them to grow.

Our offense separates us from a holy God, yet this same God gives us a way back into a right relationship. And then He invites us to join Him on the mission of bringing other wayward children home. We need the Lord's help to fulfill our purpose.

A Walk With Adam – The Lie Believed

> "For God doth know that in the day ye eat thereof, then your eyes shall be opened, and ye shall be as gods, knowing good and evil. And when the woman saw that

the tree was good for food, and that it was pleasant to the eyes, and a tree to be desired to make one wise, she took of the fruit thereof, and did eat, and gave also unto her husband with her; and he did eat. And the eyes of them both were opened, and they knew that they were naked; and they sewed fig leaves together, and made themselves aprons…So he drove out the man; and he placed at the east of the garden of Eden Cherubims, and a flaming sword which turned every way, to keep the way of the tree of life." – **Genesis 3:6-7, 24 KJV**

Many have read the account of Adam and Eve and said, they had it all, why did they believe the serpent? Why did they eat the one fruit they could not have, when there was so much they could have? As much as we ask that question, we really need to ask ourselves the same type of question. Why do we go after the one thing we cannot have, when there is so much we can? Why do we believe the lies of the enemy when God's truth is right there before us?

Adam and Eve believed one of the biggest lies, that they could become god. The fruit of that lie looked good, but it brought bitterness to their lives and soul. Man was created for greatness but he lost that place. Man was created good, but his disobedience totally destroyed his place and allowed corruption into what God had said was good.

When Adam and Eve ate of the fruit, they disobeyed God and their disobedience moved them from the presence of God. The place that God had created for mankind was now off limits to them. They were now aware of their nakedness (their shame) before God. God in his love covered it. This was a simple act, yet it foreshadows for us that it is only God that can cover up man's shame, for man is not capable of doing it.

All mankind lost this place of standing with the Lord because of the offense of Adam's disobedience. No man born is able to stand before this Holy God. I've heard people say, it's not fair that we are guilty because of Adam's sin. Yet, I must interject, if it were you or I, we most likely would still be in the same place (if not worse), because we make the same types of choices today. God's law gives specific details on what men must do, yet we break that law. We are not able to keep it, so we stand just as Adam, guilty of disobedience. We stand as an offender because we believe the lie that we can be god. We believe we can decide our own way, and can create our own truth.

The lie Adam and Eve believed is very similar to our wrong beliefs. We believe that what is out of reach or forbidden is in some way better than what God has allowed or given to us. We don't see these restrictions as the work of a loving Father, but we believe the lie that God is withholding something good from us.

We need to ask God to help us see the truth and not give in to the temptation of accepting the lies that come to separate us from a Holy God. I pray for us to learn to be patient and trust God's process. And finally, I pray that we ask God to give us a deeper discernment to help us uncover the deceptive lies sent to get us out of God's will.

A Walk With Adam – Lawbreakers

> "For whosoever shall keep the whole law and yet offend in one point, he is guilty of all. For he that said, Do not commit adultery, said also, Do not kill. Now if thou commit no adultery, yet if thou kill, thou art become a transgressor of the law." – **James 2:10-11 KJV**

We know that all men are born into sin as the Scripture confirms because of Adam's disobedience. Yet this is not the only reason why we are separated from God. God gave His people, the Israelites the Ten Commandments (as well as other Laws they were required to observe). Many think the Law was something that could be kept, but historically the Bible shows man was never able to keep all of God's law. And the truth is, when you break one law, you are called a lawbreaker.

People believe if I keep the Ten Commandments, then I should be able to live with God, I am good. The book of James tells us differently. If you break one of the laws, you become guilty of all. Have you ever lied? Even a little one? Have you ever had someone answer your phone and you tell them to say you were not at home, but you were? That means you lied. That makes you a liar and a lawbreaker. Have you ever taken something that wasn't yours, even if it happened when you were a kid? That makes you a thief and a lawbreaker. Those offenses are upon your head. If you were able to keep almost all the commandments, but were guilty only in one, you are a lawbreaker and a transgressor of the Law. You or I could not go to court and tell the judge, I only broke one law but I kept all the rest, so I should be released. The judge would tell you that you are guilty and sentence you to time for the offense.

So we stand guilty because of Adam's transgression AND we are guilty because of the sins we commit ourselves. So where can we turn? We are lawbreakers and we have the sentence of death upon our heads. Who will stand for me? Who will stand for you? Christ is the answer to this tension in life. We can walk in our purpose when we accept the gift of salvation through Christ. Adam shows us our condition to lead us to our answer.

I pray for us today that we examine ourselves. Are we guilty of breaking God's Law? Are we standing before Him as lawbreakers, or have we found the path to a pardon? God is the only one that can forgive us of the offense we have committed against Him.

A Walk With Adam – From Death to Life

> "Nevertheless death reigned from Adam to Moses, even over them that had not sinned after the similitude of Adam's transgression, who is the figure of him that was to come. But not as the offence, so also is the free gift. For if through the offence of one many be dead, much more the grace of God, and the gift by grace, which is by one man, Jesus Christ, hath abounded unto many. And not as it was by one that sinned, so is the gift: for the judgment was by one to condemnation, but the free gift is of many

offences unto justification. For if by one man's offence death reigned by one; much more they which receive abundance of grace and of the gift of righteousness shall reign in life by one, Jesus Christ." – **Romans 5:14-17 KJV**

God created man for greatness but man transgressed and forfeited what God had for him. Man (Adam) gave up his place of honor and divine purpose. God was also offended by all men's willful sin against His Holy Law. And when I say offended, I mean slighted or snubbed. Humanity had the audacity to disregard God's requirements.

Sin was not a surprise to God. Before Adam's transgression, the cross was on the heart of God. Before the first Law was engraved on tablets, the cross was in God's eyesight. We sometimes only look at Jesus when we think about our sins, but we must not forget that God through Jesus provided our way of escape. It was the entire Triune God at work in the deliverance of mankind. When God first said "let us create man in our image," He already had agreement from all (Father, Son and Holy Spirit). The Triune God not only created men, but created a plan to return mankind back to the original plan. God already knew what sin would do and that men could not help themselves on their own.

All men were destined to die because of one, but God through one, Jesus Christ would live. Men are taken from death to life because of the gift of God. God was offended by our sins, yet He did not allow our offense to stop Him from loving us. Our offense did not stop God from creating a bridge over the great cavern of sin that keeps us separated from Him. Imagine if someone offends you. A husband or wife who has an unfaithful spouse would turn from the offending party. Even if forgiveness is given, the relationship has been broken and may never be the same. Yet God, whom we have offended, says He is still "married" to us, He is married to the backslider. He not only forgives the offense, but God also provides all that is necessary to remove the mark of it. On top of that (as if that isn't great enough) God gives His Spirit to help us so we can succeed over the old self that tries to call us back into the offense of the former life.

What a great gift we have been given. God knows that we can't save ourselves, and in spite of our offense against Him; God provides all that is needed for us to reconcile our relationship to Him. Oh wretched man that I am, why would God be mindful of me? It can only be because God loves me more than I could love myself.

A Walk With Adam – Man's Purpose Regained

> "Therefore being justified by faith, we have peace with God through our Lord Jesus Christ: By whom also we have access by faith into this grace wherein we stand, and rejoice in hope of the glory of God. And not only so, but we glory in tribulations also: knowing that tribulation worketh patience; and patience, experience; and experience, hope: And hope maketh not ashamed; because the love of God is shed abroad in our hearts by

the Holy Ghost which is given unto us. For when we were yet without strength, in due time Christ died for the ungodly. For scarcely for a righteous man will one die: yet peradventure for a good man some would even dare to die. But God commandeth his love toward us, in that, while we were yet sinners, Christ died for us. Much more then, being now justified by his blood, we shall be saved from wrath through him." – **Romans 5:1-9 KJV**

We no longer have to be separated from God because of our sins; we can be justified by faith in Christ. We cannot work towards salvation, but it is a free gift that we can only access when we take hold of it through faith in Christ. No sin is too big that God cannot forgive and no sin is too small that it does not need forgiveness.

We can also rejoice because God will take our tribulations and work them to grow us. It brings forth patience and experience and through that experience with God, we gain hope. We are not ashamed because the love of God is in our hearts and the Holy Ghost bears witness to our hearts that we belong to God.

At the right time when we were weak, Christ died for the ungodly. God's love was strong enough to present His Son as a living sacrifice for all. His love was strong enough to give the blood of His Son as a perfect lamb sacrifice to cover all sins for all humanity. God's power is still strong enough. The question is, are we accepting the gift offered to us?

God offers to all a way of escaping the wrath due to all sinners by accepting His Son's offer of salvation. When we accept the gift of love from God, the one we offended, we can regain the purpose God had when He first said, let us create man in our image. We can go from the old Adam, the lawbreaker, to walking like the new Adam, the fulfiller of the Law, Jesus. No, we aren't the savior, but we have access to His power to help us walk in the fulfillment of purpose.

God purposed in His heart that men would reflect His attributes. Man's purpose was to honor and praise God. Man's purpose was to have fellowship with God. Man's purpose was to bring forth fruit and bring others to the likeness of God. We could not fulfill this purpose in our lives, because we had forfeited it to sin's control. We could not be good no matter how much we wanted to be good. What we knew to do, we could not because of flesh's control. We could not gain control over the flesh, without God's Spirit equipping us to do it.

We can take back the purpose we were intended to fulfill from the beginning. We can be lovers of God because God fills us with His love. We cannot even love God, without His help and power. We can give praise to God, because God has filled our hearts with a joy that expresses itself in a hope that is only attainable because God first gave it to us. We offended God, yet He did not leave us there. He loved us enough to turn the offense around onto himself. He took the punishment that we deserved for the offense that was against Him! My God, You took the bruising for our sins that was administered by our own hands. Help us to realize what You truly did for us on Calvary. We must humbly submit ourselves to God to cleanse us, equip us, and help us to become what He wanted when He saw man and said, it is very good.

Life Lessons

A walk through the life of Adam is one in recognition of who we are as people. Adam and Eve's one choice opened a door they could not close. They went from walking in God's presence to experiencing fear (hiding from God), fault finding (it was her fault or his fault), and more.

They believed that by eating they could become god-like, the truth was they were already like God. Notice the difference. They weren't gods, but they had the attributes of God making them like Him and giving them access to do all that He had for them. We must be careful today not to allow our walk in life to lead us to places where we feed that lie of being god. When we do it brings destruction. Yet we are grateful we have a way to get from under this destruction, and that's through Christ.

Our offense doesn't have to keep us separated from God. When we acknowledge it and seek the love of the Father offered through Jesus Christ, we can go from separated to set apart for His good works. It seems impossible to understand how an enemy of God can become His trusted servant. But that is how much God loves us.

CHARACTER ON DISPLAY

THE PROPHETS were the ones God chose to speak for Him by communicating His message. The prophet had to be courageous because the messages given weren't always well received. The prophets received their call or appointment to the office of the prophet directly by God.

Some were called before birth (like Jeremiah and John the Baptist, Jer. 2:5; Luke 1:13-16). Except for God's call, the prophets had no special qualifications; other than obedience to the One who called. Some prophets were called for a lifetime, but sometimes they were called for a specific assignment. Whatever the assignment of the prophet, it was always to draw people to God and to raise them up to the level of life God had for them. Additionally, the prophet was required to display the attributes, the character of God.

A Walk With Daniel – Daniel's story

> "Then king Darius wrote unto all people, nations, and languages, that dwell in all the earth; Peace be multiplied unto you. I make a decree, That in every dominion of my kingdom men tremble and fear before the God of Daniel: for he is the living God, and steadfast for ever, and his kingdom that which shall not be destroyed, and his dominion shall be ever unto the end. He delievereth and

rescueth, and he worketh signs and wonders in heaven and in earth, who hath delivered Daniel from the power of the lions." – **Daniel 6:26-28 KJV**

In the context of the Scripture, Daniel found favor with the king and he put him in a high place of honor. However, there were those who Daniel ranked over that plotted to destroy him. They couldn't find anything wrong with his character, so they devised a plan to destroy him with his worship of God. One important characteristic of those called to speak for God is to make sure our integrity speaks honorably of us.

These men planned a plot concerning Daniel's worship to try and have him killed. They convinced the king that anyone worshiping anything other than him shouldn't be trusted. This plot led to the king passing a decree that anyone praying to any god or man for the next thirty days would be thrown into the lion's den.

Daniel heard the decree, but he didn't stop his daily worship. Another important characteristic necessary in the people of God is the courage to stand in the face of adversity; even if it means trouble for obeying God. Because Daniel didn't stop praying, he was arrested and thrown into the lion's den. Yet the story doesn't tragically end there. God sent an angel and shut up the mouth of the lions and saved Daniel from destruction. Darius had all those that sought to destroy Daniel along with their families thrown into the lion dean. Darius then makes this decree after God had delivered Daniel.

What is the importance of this for us today? When we live for the Lord the enemy doesn't want to see us succeed. We know the enemy is waiting to destroy and he will use anyone to get us off track. They counted Daniel out of the game. They closed him in the lion's den with a huge stone; they left him for dead. However, that wasn't the end of Daniel's story. God had another plan for Daniel. This lion's den wasn't going to be his tomb! This den condition wasn't going to be Daniel's last situation or the one that would kill his purpose

Daniel had to trust God to save him. Even though he didn't have any guarantees about how God would respond, Daniel was willing to count the cost. Another characteristic necessary in the heart of the believer is the willingness to trust even when we have no way of knowing how something will work out.

Daniel was rescued and because of his faith in God it resulted in the king decreeing that Daniel's God was the true God. When we stand strong through our adversities, we stand in the position of others decreeing that God is the true God because of how they saw Him show up in our lives.

A Walk with Jeremiah – Jeremiah's Story

> "Then took they Jeremiah, and cast him into the dungeon of Malchiah the son of Hammelech, that was in the court of the prison; and they let down Jeremiah with cords. And in the dungeon there was no water, but mire: so Jeremiah sunk in the mire. Now when Ebedmelech the Ethiopian,

one of the eunuchs which was in the king's house, heard that they had put Jeremiah in the dungeon; the king then sitting in the gate of Benjamin; Ebedmelech went forth out of the kings house, and spake to the king, saying, My lord the king, these men have done evil in all that they have done to Jeremiah the prophet, whom they have cast into the dungeon; and he is like to die for hunger in the place where he is; for there is no more bread in the city. Then the king commanded Ebedmelech the Ethiopian saying, Take from hence thirty men with thee, and take up Jeremiah the prophet out of the dungeon, before he die." – **Jeremiah 38:6-10 KJV**

Jeremiah had been a faithful servant to God. He stood for God and spoke the word of God even when they wanted to kill him. Whenever the Lord said go, Jeremiah went. He went to the people, to the priest, prophets and kings. Whomever God said give a message to, Jeremiah did it. Yet the people plotted to destroy Jeremiah, because they didn't want to hear God's truth. One thing necessary for the prophet to realize is the message, though good for people isn't always accepted by them.

The people had "tickling ears" and they wanted to hear messages they liked, not what was beneficial to them. In his walk, Jeremiah was faced with many difficulties, yet God kept him. Here is one of those situations. Jeremiah had spoken to the people but a group of men were tired of Jeremiah, so they took him and put him into a dungeon. They lowered Jeremiah in the pit and he began to sink in the mud. They were expecting this to be the end of Jeremiah. People will try to shut up the prophet but we must continue to speak.

Though Jeremiah was in this situation; God touched the heart of the king's servant Ebedmelech, and had him request Jeremiah's release. Ebedmelech went and got Jeremiah from the dungeon. He took great care getting him out. Ebedmelech's name means "servant of the king". Yes, he was the servant to the earthly king, but he also became the servant to the Heavenly King; used to raise Jeremiah up from what was meant to be his death.

God may want to use you as His servant, an Ebemelech, to pull someone from the condition trying to pull them under. It is important for us to be intercessors for those who are the frontline of the faith. While this story is about Jeremiah, it is key for us to understand that the prophets need some Ebemelechs in their lives willing to help them by interceding for them. He may also want to use you to be the one to reach out and pull those sinking in sin to a place of rescue. Additionally, we can see that God also wants us to be willing to go on rescue missions for those lost in sin because of their choices. We need to seek God's direction to be equipped as a servant of the king ready to reach out with tenderness and give a helping hand to someone sinking fast, especially those who are doing the Lord's business.

> "Then the word of the LORD came unto me saying, Before I formed thee in the belly I knew thee; and before thou camest forth out of the womb I sanctified thee, and I ordained thee a prophet unto the nations. Then said I, Ah, Lord God! Behold, I cannot speak; for I am a child. But the LORD said unto me, Say not, I am a child: for thou shalt go to all that I shall send thee and whatsoever I command thee thou shalt speak. Be not afraid of their faces; for I am with thee to deliver thee, said the LORD."
> – **Jeremiah 1:4-8 KJV**

In this passage, Jeremiah is also getting a message similar to what Ezekiel received. God tells Jeremiah He knew him and had a purpose for his life even before he was born. This is a great reason for why we should look at the unborn child differently than our society tells us. The thought has crossed my mind, are we killing those who could bring about the cure for cancer, or the next Billy Graham or someone that has a great purpose for God? The truth is, only God knows what He has planted in the life of the unborn.

Jeremiah gave his reasons to God why he didn't feel qualified to speak. Jeremiah said he was too young. Yet God knows who He wants to use and in what manner. We only have to allow Him access. Sometimes we are afraid, not just because of physical age, but also due to spiritual immaturity. We need not worry. God can give us what we need to complete the task. He gives Jeremiah the encouragement not to worry about the faces of the people. God also tells Jeremiah, don't be afraid of them because He would deliver him from them. And Jeremiah learned over time to trust this promise from God as he continued to carry the message. We too must learn to trust the promises of God to help us carry out the assignment on our lives.

God sets a purpose for us; and for some, even before we came into the earth. The Scripture says He sanctified thee. He set us aside for a special purpose. Jeremiah was called from the womb, but his fears made him want to disqualify himself. We can't allow our limitations to stop us from accepting who God called us to be. He called, He will equip.

Whatever the assignment, He will equip us to fulfill. If it's a mother of four, God has all you need to complete that ministry. If it's a husband trying to take care of his family God has all you need to complete the task. Are you a Sunday school teacher trying to teach to unyielding ears? Teach on! God has all you need.

A Walk With Ezekiel – Ezekiel's Story

> "And he said unto me, Son of man, I send thee to the children of Israel, to a rebellious nation that hath rebelled against me: they and their fathers have transgressed against me, even unto this very day. For they are impudent children and stiffnecked. I do send thee unto them; and thou shalt say unto

them, Thus saith the Lord God. And they, whether they will hear, or whether they will forbear, (for they are a rebellious house,) yet shall know that there hath been a prophet among them. And thou, son of man, be not afraid of them, neither be afraid of their words, though briers and thorns be with thee, and thou dost dwell among scorpions: be not afraid of their words, nor be dismayed at their looks, though they be a rebellious house. But thou, son of man, hear what I say unto thee; Be not thou rebellious like that rebellious house: open thy mouth, and eat that I give thee. " – **Ezekiel 2:3-8 KJV**

God calls for His people to be willing to make a stand for Him. Here God calls Ezekiel to give His word to the rebellious children of Israel that are in captivity in Babylon. They have refused to turn and yet God is sending Ezekiel to them. He tells him I know they are hardheaded, I know that I'm sending you to those that don't want to listen. *Go anyway*.

God tells Ezekiel, do not be afraid of the people. Don't worry about their faces or what they look like. Don't worry about their words of discouragement or bitterness. Don't worry about their complaining or troublemaking. God tells Ezekiel, don't worry about their lies or their destructive ways. Don't worry about them. Just go and say as I tell you to say. He also says, you make sure you are obeying me.

Even if it gets discouraging and seems as if we are all alone on our walk, we are not. We have a true friend with us, Jesus. The message is clear. We have to go as the Lord instructs us. Some may say, this doesn't apply to me, I wasn't called to preach. Maybe not, but we were all called to be "living sacrifices, which is our reasonable service unto the Lord" (Romans 12:1). Being a living sacrifice means we give God the right to use us as He wishes. He may tell us to correct an error or to tell someone in a hostile environment about Him. He says, don't worry what they look like. You just tell them what I say. We can do this when we allow Him to build a character of trust and strength in us. We trust Him, so we obey Him.

God knows beforehand who He is sending us to face. He knows the heart condition of the people. Yet because He is a loving God, He still wants ALL to have an opportunity to hear the truth. We have to be willing to put all on the line for the mission of our great God.

We must hold His hand and know that where He sends us, we can follow. And let us be mindful to keep our focus on Him and not at those around us.

A Walk With Samuel – Samuel's Story

> "And it came to pass, when they were come, that he looked on Eliab, and said, surely the LORD'S anointed is before him. But the LORD said unto Samuel, look not on his countenance, or on the height of his stature; because I have refused him; for the LORD looketh on the heart." –
> **1 Samuel 16:6-7 KJV**

When Saul had disobeyed God, he sent Samuel to anoint a new king. Samuel went to Jesse's family and began by looking at the biggest of his sons and thought this must be the one. Yet God said no. Samuel went through all of Jesse's sons until he came to David, the smallest of them. And this is who God wanted anointed. Samuel made the mistake that many of us make, we look at outward manifestations [such as size, or talent, or performance] but God looks inwardly [the heart]. God is calling for the prophet [all believers] to remember to seek Him when making decisions to ensure that our humanity isn't making the choice; the choice is God's.

This is a great reminder to us that we can't say, well I'm only a teacher, or I'm only a singer in the choir, so God couldn't want me. God doesn't look at our list of credentials or what things man looks at. God looks at the heart condition of man. We must stop disqualifying ourselves from God's mission because of things we think are too great to overcome. God doesn't look at our lack, but our willingness of heart. He will do the building in us to equip us for the job.

God is looking for willing vessels to carry out His purpose. I don't know about you, but I don't want to be one God refuses to use. I want my heart to be available to God without excuses. I want to be willing to seek Him and to hear when He calls. I want to say yes Lord, to His will. David didn't refuse to allow Samuel to anoint him for the next assignment in his life. We must not refuse to allow God's servant to prepare us for our next. And if we are the Samuel, we must be willing to hear God's instruction clearly to prepare the ones God sends us to rise up for their next.

Life Lessons

While God doesn't call all to be prophets, we can still learn much about how we are to live our lives before God. He called the prophets to be integral to His word. He required them to give His message whether it was well received or not. He mandated that the prophets be ready to face whatever adversity that came for the sake of God. This mandate is the same for all followers of Jesus Christ. We are required to handle the word of God with care. Whether we handle it through teaching, preaching or living it, we must align our lives to following the instructions of God.

The prophets had to make sure they were moving based on God's requirements and not their ideas. We are required not to look at outward things when making godly decisions; but to seek God. To follow this mandate requires us to learn to tune our spiritual ears to hear God clearly.

And the prophets had to endure the difficulties that arose because they were obedient to God's mandates. Today, we can feel discouraged or unprotected when faced with difficulties. Yet, we must remember that these things will come, but God has some servants positioned to help us by praying for us and interceding on our behalf. We must stay true to the assignment and allow God to continue to build our character.

THE UNNAMED MOTHER

THE UNNAMED MOTHER isn't stated, but I can visualize her presence. The Scripture doesn't actually mention the mother, only the lad with the lunch. However, I take the liberty here that there was a mother who provided the young boy with the things he needed, even if he made the lunch himself.

Why is this assumption important? I often notice in Scripture that we have deeds shown by people without always telling us who they were or any background information about them. Yet, there is still a valuable lesson in it. For example, how many know who Billy Graham's Sunday school teacher was or the name of one of his mentors? Not many, but they were valuable to Billy Graham's story. There are some unnamed mothers and fathers that have made a difference in who others have become.

A Walk with the Unnamed Mother - Who Made the Lunch?

> There is a lad here, which hath five barley loaves, and two small fishes: but what are they among so many? And Jesus said, Make the men sit down. Now there was much grass in the place. So the men sat down, in number about five thousand. And Jesus took the loaves; and when he had given thanks, he distributed to the disciples, and the

disciples to them that were sat down; and likewise of the fishes as much as they would. When they were filled, he said unto his disciples, Gather up the fragments that remain, that nothing be lost. – **John 6:9-12 KJV**

We have probably heard this Scripture spoken on many times, but it has either been from the perspective of Jesus performing the miracle or the boy's willingness to give his lunch, but what if he didn't have any lunch to give?

There was a mother who we do not have the name of that took the time to make this lunch for her son. It also strikes me that she knew where he was going and she wanted him to have something to keep him nourished while he was there. First let's look at the fact that this mother knew where he was going. The news of Jesus was known among the people, that is why the multitudes came to hear him and see the miracles, in hopes that they would receive one. This mother allowed her son to go to where Jesus was. So this mother was not only looking out for the physical need of her son, but she was trying to look out for the spiritual need as well.

I state clearly, the Scripture doesn't tell us this is true, but I take a few liberties based on family life and the context of the Scripture. The lesson we can glean is as a parent, it is important that we willing take care of our children's needs. We must make sure that they are receiving sustenance for their physical body, but more importantly we need to make sure they are being taken to places where Jesus' presence is there.

We are responsible for the care of our children's spiritual development (parents in general) and we must do all we can to make sure they are in the right places so they can hear the word and see the miracles that Jesus still does today.

The question we must ask ourselves daily is am I preparing the right type of meal for my children? We need to make sure they are fed physically, but more importantly spiritually. We need the Lord to help us to make sure we give our children something of substance, but that means we must first have something to give. So we need God to work in us so we can have something to give to our children.

A Walk With the Unnamed Mother - Prepare for Miracles

> There is a lad here, which hath five barley loaves, and two small fishes: but what are they among so many? And Jesus said, Make the men sit down. Now there was much grass in the place. So the men sat down, in number about five thousand. And Jesus took the loaves; and when he had given thanks, he distributed to the disciples, and the disciples to them that were sat down; and likewise of the fishes as much as they would. When they were filled, he said unto his disciples, Gather up the fragments that remain, that nothing be lost. – **John 6:9-12 KJV**

This unnamed mother sent her son out with five loaves and two small fish, which may seem to have been only enough for him, but Jesus shows differently. When Jesus tells the disciples to give the over five thousand (because this number only lists the men) something to eat, they are perplexed. They don't have enough money to provide for all these people. They surely didn't bring enough to give the people to eat. Then someone remembers the one boy that had the five loaves and two small fishes.

Let me stop here for a moment. How was this boy picked out of all those that were there? Tell me, how easy is it to find one person among over 5,000 people? So in my mind, some kind of way, this lad must have made himself available with what he had. He had to have let someone know he had something to add, even if it was just a little.

This mother, when she prepared this lunch for her son, may not have known she was preparing him to become part of a miracle, yet that is just what she did. This should be an encouragement to us that while we prepare our children, we don't know what miracle God wants to do through their life, but we should prepare them for the process. Jesus took that small amount that the boy had and multiplied it so that not only was it enough to feed those there, but there were fragments left over.

This is a message for us today, we need to plant in our children those things that will help them to have a willingness to offer themselves to the work of God. This young boy willingly gave his lunch to Jesus, he didn't say, hey, if I give you what I have, I won't have anything. Instead, he gave. So it is our responsibility as parents [natural and spiritual] to help our children have a willingness to serve the Lord. And it is important that they see that in us first. What a blessing to know that what we feed our children can be used to feed others!

A Walk With the Unnamed Mother - Prepare Your Child to Stand Out
> There is a lad here, which hath five barley loaves, and two small fishes: but what are they among so many? And Jesus said, Make the men sit down. Now there was much grass in the place. So the men sat down, in number about five thousand. And Jesus took the loaves; and when he had given thanks, he distributed to the disciples, and the disciples to them that were sat down; and likewise of the fishes as much as they would. When they were filled, he said unto his disciples, Gather up the fragments that remain, that nothing be lost. – **John 6:9-12 KJV**

I want to go back to the point about how the lad was seen in the midst of the over 5,000 people. I still cannot imagine how someone was able to spot this boy among many. What made him different? Surely there had to be other boys there. Surely he wasn't so tall that he stood above the others (like Saul did and that's why they picked him as king). So what made him different?

Allow my mind a few moments of wondering if you will. The one thing we can see that made him stand out, is that he came prepared. His mother didn't know how long her son would be gone, it could have been a long time on this journey, and she wanted to ensure her child was fed. She was thinking ahead. The fact that the rest of the crowd was in need of food, means they did not come prepared for this part of the journey.

When this mother sent her son out into the mass of people, she sent him out differently. He was prepared to stand out in this crowd. How did the news get to the disciples? Was this boy close to them or was he far away in the crowd? This information we do not have, yet we can know for sure that he was part of a bigger plan for that day. We do not always know how things work behind the scenes, but we are able to see the outcome. It is the same way in our spiritual life, we do not always see the workings of the Spirit and how He works events to serve God's plan, but we can see the outcome of His working in our lives. He brings things together to work the way the Lord has ordained it to work.

This young boy had an appointed time to stand out and in doing so; God is given the glory for it. This young boy is not the one that deserves the glory, but God was glorified through his obedience and sacrifice. This young man stood out in the crowd so that Jesus could shine. We can also make some assumptions about this boy; he had been taught to be respectful to his elders. We don't see any resistance to the request to give up his lunch. How we train up our children is important to how they show up in situations when we aren't around them.

As parents, that is what we are called to do, prepare our children for their moment to be called out of the crowd so that Jesus can shine through their sacrifices and obedience. We prepare them to do that when we send them on their journey with the provisions that will sustain them.

And we can know that it will not only sustain them, but God will use it to feed others.

We must feed our children the word of God and make sure that when they go out on their journeys in life, that they are ready to feed not only themselves, but to feed the multitudes they will encounter. When we prepare them, we are preparing them for greatness in the Lord. Preparing our children for the journey will someday result in them taking their place in history (God's story) and standing out in the crowd so that Jesus can be glorified.

A Walk With the Unnamed Mother - Prepare Your Children to Have a Testimony

> There is a lad here, which hath five barley loaves, and two small fishes: but what are they among so many? And Jesus said, Make the men sit down. Now there was much grass in the place. So the men sat down, in number about five thousand. And Jesus took the loaves; and when he had given thanks, he distributed to the disciples, and the disciples to them that were sat down; and likewise of the fishes as much as they would. When they were filled, he said unto his disciples, Gather up the fragments that remain, that nothing be lost. – **John 6:9-12 KJV**

Why did this mother allow her son to go to where Jesus was? It could have been because she had heard of all the miracles and wonders of Jesus. It could have been because she wanted her son to experience Jesus' miracles first hand, and not only have his deeds told of by someone else. She may have wanted her son to have a true experience with this man named Jesus.

This mother allowed her son to have an encounter with Jesus, to find something out about Him, but he went and got something so much more. Again we do not know where he was in the crowd in relation to where Jesus was, but we do know that he was able to come closer to Him, because Jesus needed his lunch.

We do not know if Jesus took the lunch from the boy or if he got it from the disciples, but whatever it was, the boy was close enough to feel the presence of Jesus. He was close enough to see Jesus take the little he had and bless it. He was close enough to see the many fed with his small lunch with much left over.

This lad was able to go back home and tell those that didn't come about the miracles of Jesus. Not because someone told him, but because he experienced them himself. He had a testimony about the wonder-working powers of Jesus.

This reminds us today that we must prepare our children to have a testimony about the Savior. We do that first by the example we set within the privacy of our own homes. Do our children see us living out our salvation in such a way that they know Jesus is real? Do we show them Jesus' miracles within our lives?

We must prepare our children to have a testimony of how Jesus can save, change, deliver, restore and so much more. We do this by sending them to the presence of Jesus. We send them, because Jesus needs what they have inside, He wants to use them just like He wants to use us. We send them, maybe expecting a simple encounter, but we should pray for an up close and personal relationship. We should pray that God allows them to experience a true relationship with Christ, so that when they are asked "who is this Jesus," they will be ready to give an answer of what they believed because it is what they have experienced themselves.

A Walk With the Unnamed Mother - Prepare Your Child's

> There is a lad here, which hath five barley loaves, and two small fishes: but what are they among so many? And Jesus said, Make the men sit down. Now there was much grass in the place. So the men sat down, in number about five thousand. And Jesus took the loaves; and when he had given thanks, he distributed to the disciples, and the disciples to them that were sat down; and likewise of the fishes as much as they would. When they were filled, he said unto his disciples, Gather up the fragments that remain, that nothing be lost. – **John 6:9-12 KJV**

This story, while short in content, is not small in application or meaning. We first talked about who made the lunch, focusing on this mother that is left unnamed, and what her value is to her son. This unnamed mother was preparing her son for a miracle. She was preparing him to stand out in the crowd and she was preparing him to have a testimony, all by preparing his lunch that day.

Have you ever thought, that as you send your child out the door today on what seems to be an ordinary day, that something extraordinary may happen (this can also apply to ourselves)? This may be the day that what you prepared for them, will give them the opportunity to stand out in the crowd as they experience a miracle of the Lord, which will give them a testimony to share with others.

This unnamed mother was preparing her son to be used for the purpose of God. This lad's lunch did not seem like much, that is what the disciples said, "But what are they among so many?" The disciples did not understand something very important, that God can multiply from the little we have to offer. This disciple was not trying to discourage anyone, but could have done so by his words.

Sometimes we look at our children, and what we see may not seem like a lot, so we do not encourage them to use their abilities. But we must remember that even the little bit in the hands of the Lord can be used mightily.

We should encourage our children to use what they have. These few loaves and fish really were not enough to feed the over 5,000. But God's math is AWESOME! He can take the small that was enough for only one and feed the multitude and still have some left over. Who can do that other than God?

We need God to help us prepare our children to be used by Him, even where they are at now. We should not be waiting until they have what we think is enough, but teach them how to give what is inside of them NOW. If they like to sing, have them sing with the children's choir, it doesn't matter if they are the best singer or not, just let them learn to give praises to God. Whatever they like to do, teach them how this small thing can be used by God to bless many. Let us seek God for how we can do just as this unnamed mother did, prepare our children to be a blessing to others through the offering of what has been given to them. We need to help them to feed others, just as they have been fed.

Life Lessons

Again, I acknowledge the Scripture doesn't specifically tell us who made this lunch for the young boy. In fact, he could have done it himself. Yet, even in that, a parent still provides the items for him to make the lunch. Someone had to have taught him how to prepare a lunch.

However you work this out, the lad had the help and support of a family; a mother and/or father. Someone had to teach him the things that allowed him to be comfortable in the midst of this crowd. And that is the lesson we want to remember; we need to make sure we are investing in our children [natural and spiritual] to make sure they are ready when God calls for them to step up and be used.

And as that parent, we must be fine if we stay in the background, unknown by name, but we are not unknown by our deeds. Too often we can get caught up in trying to live through the experiences and success of our children. That's not what we want to do. As a loving parent, we prepare them and then step aside and give God access to use them for His glory. As a parent our reward is that we prepared them well.

THE MESSAGE

JEREMIAH was a major prophet during the decline and fall of the southern kingdom of Judah. He prophesied during the reigns of the last five kings of Judah. His call was declared by God that he had sanctioned him as a prophet even before he was born (Jer. 1:5).

Yet, Jeremiah's call was not met with excitement but with an excuse for why he wasn't qualified to do it. However, God reassured Jeremiah that His calling wasn't based on Jeremiah's ability but on God's choice.

Jeremiah is often called the weeping prophet [my nickname as well] because he wept openly about the sins of the nation (Jer. 9:1). From that very moment of his calling, Jeremiah had the assignment that his words were to be God's word. His message was God's to root out, to pull down, to destroy and to throw down, to build and to plant (Jer. 1:10). Jeremiah teaches us that the prophet doesn't determine the message, God does.

Jeremiah, like many of the other prophets, had to accept their calling and be ready to speak God's message His way. Isaiah, Jonah, and Nahum all had to hear God's specific instruction for them to be enabled to accept the call, walk in the call, and not allow the outcomes to determine their future. Jonah became angry because God offered mercy, yet that is not up to the servant but the one sending the message.

A Walk With the Prophet Jeremiah – God Calls

> ⁴ The Lord gave me this message: ⁵ "I knew you before I formed you in your mother's womb. Before you were born I set you apart and appointed you as my prophet to the nations." ⁶ "O Sovereign Lord," I said, "I can't speak for you! I'm too young!" ⁷ The Lord replied, "Don't say, 'I'm too young,' for you must go wherever I send you and say whatever I tell you. ⁸ And don't be afraid of the people, for I will be with you and will protect you. I, the Lord, have spoken!" ⁹ Then the Lord reached out and touched my mouth and said, "Look, I have put my words in your mouth! ¹⁰ Today I appoint you to stand up against nations and kingdoms. Some you must uproot and tear down, destroy and overthrow. Others you must build up and plant." – **Jeremiah 1:4-10 NLT**

This is the calling of the prophet Jeremiah. The Lord is speaking to Jeremiah and reassuring him that he was formed in his mother's womb with a purpose. That purpose was for him to be a prophet to the nations. Jeremiah's response isn't much different from others (such as Moses) when called for such an awesome task.

His response is, But God I cannot speak. I am only a child. Maybe our response isn't the same as Jeremiah's, but we can relate. Maybe your response to God when He spoke His purpose to you was, "I can't do that," or "Will people listen to me?" or even, "I don't know enough, I'm not good enough.: Whatever the excuse is, God's answer to us is the same as it was to Jeremiah.

God told Jeremiah, do not say you are a child, but you must go and speak everything I command you to say. Do not be afraid to speak the words I give you for I will rescue you. In other words, I will be with you as you speak the words I give you to speak.

Then God reached out and touched Jeremiah's lips and said, I now put my words into your mouth, so go forth and do as I have commanded. God's word comes through us to uproot and tear down those attitudes, behaviors and beliefs that would set themselves up above God. God's word also comes to build up and to plant, to build up His people for the fight ahead and to plant the good seed that will take root and bring forth fruit.

Today, God is calling. He is calling for His people to step forth and walk in the truth as He sets forth. He is calling His people to pick up their armor and begin to run this race, His way. We must allow the truth of God's word to set us free from the sins that so easily beset us. God has a message for us, are we listening?

A Walk With the Prophet Isaiah – God Promises

> [13] Then Isaiah said, "Listen well, you royal family of David! Isn't it enough to exhaust human patience? Must you exhaust the patience of my God as well? [14] All right then, the Lord himself will give you the sign. Look! The virgin will conceive a child! She will give birth to a son

and will call him Immanuel (which means 'God is with us'). ¹⁵ By the time this child is old enough to choose what is right and reject what is wrong, he will be eating yogurt and honey. ¹⁶ For before the child is that old, the lands of the two kings you fear so much will both be deserted. ¹⁷ "Then the Lord will bring things on you, your nation, and your family unlike anything since Israel broke away from Judah. He will bring the king of Assyria upon you!"– **Isaiah 7:13-17 NLT**

The prophet Isaiah spoke of the promise of a coming Messiah to the people of Israel. Isaiah says to the people that God would give them a sign of His promise of protection. That sign would be a virgin with child and His name would be Immanuel. The promise was a sign also regarding the breaking of the control of the two kings that were bothersome to Israel.

However, the people did not truly understand the words of the prophet, Isaiah. We know that because when Jesus did come, they were looking for a different kind of savior or messiah. They were looking for a savior that would fulfill the latter part of what Isaiah spoke. They were looking for someone to break the hold of other kingdoms over them. They were looking for a savior that would come in and set up an earthly kingdom, with physical strength and might. The people's misunderstanding of the words of the prophet does not change the words of the prophet. Isaiah's words were true because they were the words of God. And God always fulfills His word.

What is the lesson for us in this Scripture? We must listen carefully to the words of the Lord however He sends them. If He sends the message by a person, or if it comes from the very Scriptures of the Holy Bible, it must be heeded. We must listen carefully to them so that we understand what God is saying. We don't want to be like the people of Isaiah's time and misinterpret the message and lose out on the promise. Many rejected Jesus because He was not the Messiah they were looking for.

Let us not reject the truth about Jesus because He is not what we think. Let us not reject the promises of God when He sends word to us of what He is offering to us. Let us respond to the message, to the call. We must heed to the message of God so that we can hear the truth of what He is telling us. We need God to help us to hear clearly what is in His word and what He speaks through His servants. We don't want to reject Jesus, because to do so, we reject the promises for our safety and deliverance. God is speaking, are you listening?

A Walk With the Prophet Jonah – The Reluctant Servant

> [1]The Lord gave this message to Jonah son of Amittai: [2] "Get up and go to the great city of Nineveh. Announce my judgment against it because I have seen how wicked its people are." [3] But Jonah got up and went in the opposite direction to get away from the Lord. He went

down to the port of Joppa, where he found a ship leaving for Tarshish. He bought a ticket and went on board, hoping to escape from the Lord by sailing to Tarshish.–
Jonah 1:1-3 NLT

Most of us have heard the story about Jonah being in the belly of the fish. We have heard the story of Jonah's reluctance to do as God instructed him to do. Jonah's reluctance to do what God is telling him is because of the treatment they have received from the people of Nineveh.

If we look at this from our times and situation, this is what that means. God wants you to go to the person that has treated you the worse, and tell them the message of salvation. Maybe you just don't want to tell them, partly because you know if God says He will save them, He will. Your desire for your worst enemy is vengeance. Yet, we must be willing to let go of the desire for vengeance against those that hurts us, because God says vengeance is His.

So here we have Jonah, receiving a message from God to go and preach against wickedness. Instead of going as the Lord instructed it says, "He went down…" When Jonah went down to Joppa, he was also going down spiritually. For everything after this leads down for Jonah. He ran from God and he went down to Joppa. He went down into the ship and then he ended up down in the sea, and finally down in the belly of the fish for three days.

What's the message for us today? When we refuse to heed what God is telling us to do, we can expect to take a downward trip. The things we are trying to accomplish will go down. The self-promotion will go down, the activities will lead down, until finally we find ourselves trapped in a "fishy" situation. But the merciful God of heaven allows us to be trapped in some fishy situations because it is in those places He has our full attention. It is in those places that we must humble ourselves, if we ever hope to find release. We must protect our hearts to ensure we aren't reluctant to hear the word of the Lord and His instruction for our lives. God is calling, are you listening?

A Walk With the Prophet Nahum – God's Mercy

> The Lord is slow to get angry, but his power is great, and he never lets the guilty go unpunished. He displays his power in the whirlwind and the storm. The billowing clouds are the dust beneath his feet. – **Nahum 1:3 NLT**

This Scripture is regarding the sayings to Nineveh and God's anger against her. However, we can look at the words of this verse and see a message for us today. The Scripture reads that God is slow to anger. This small part of this Scripture speaks of the mercy and patience of God. We often confuse God's patience with a lack of power. The enemy fools us into believing that because God hasn't moved against our sinful behavior He is somehow powerless over our situations, and our sins. Or the enemy makes us believe our sin has gone unnoticed by

God and we have somehow fooled Him by our deeds. Yet, we are reminded that even though He is slow to anger, He is also great in power.

God shows not only His mercy upon those that trust Him, but God extends mercy even to the unsaved. Think about this. Even as one goes about their day continuing in unrighteousness, they are functioning within the mercy of God. It is God's mercy that the unrighteous are able to continue, but it is all done so that God can draw them to himself.

Even though God is slow to anger, He will not allow the deeds of the unrighteous to go on continually unchecked. God is a loving God and He seeks that all would turn to Him, but if we refuse to heed in the time He has given to us, we will have to stand before Him for the unrighteousness of our deeds.

If you find yourself in a storm, caught up in the whirlwind, just maybe it is God saying to you, "today is the day I am calling for you to yield". Did you know that if God calls you to accountability while you yet live, He is still showing you mercy? He is calling you to accountability NOW because He doesn't want you to perish. He will correct you now, so that you have the chance to change and right your relationship with Him.

There are people we know that have been living on the mercy of God, yet are refusing to obey Him. He has been extending His mercy, but He will correct us if we refuse to yield. So today, let us pray that when God calls those who are disobedient, they will hear. And then let us pray for ourselves that there be nothing hidden in our hearts that would make us disobedient to God. Let us pray that we would always yield to the will of God. God is calling, are you listening?

A Walk With the Prophet Jeremiah – God's Judgment

> 8 "'Don't be fooled into thinking that you will never suffer because the Temple is here. It's a lie! 9 Do you really think you can steal, murder, commit adultery, lie, and burn incense to Baal and all those other new gods of yours, 10 and then come here and stand before me in my Temple and chant, "We are safe!"—only to go right back to all those evils again? – **Jeremiah 7:8-10 NLT**

If you have ever read the book of Jeremiah, you know he continued to give the same type of message again and again to the people of God, yet they would not listen. Instead of listening to Jeremiah, they continued to do as they were doing.

The question Jeremiah asks in this Scripture is how long will you continue to trust in words that will not benefit you? How long will you run after things of the flesh and then come into the house of God as one that should be clean? How long will the flesh be able to rule is the question Jeremiah is asking the people of this time.

There is a message for us today in the words of this prophet. He talked about the judgment of God coming upon the people because they refused to turn to God and away from those things that were an abomination to God. Are we hearing the call today? Are we sitting

Sunday after Sunday but not really walking away with a clearer understanding of the message of God? Or a changed life?

Are we ignoring the warning signs being sent to us from a loving Father calling us into a right relationship with Him? We must seek to hear His calling to us because it is for our safety.

Life Lessons

God's messages for yesterday, are clearly messages for today. God is still calling for us to be willing to be messengers of righteousness. Just as God called Jeremiah from his mother's womb, He is calling us today. Just as God sent word of the promises of Jesus as the savior through the prophet Isaiah, those promises are still for us today. The Savior is still the Savior today. Jesus is still the only way that we can have power over the flesh so that we do not sin against God.

Let us not be like the reluctant prophet, Jonah and refuse to do as we are instructed and set ourselves up for a "downward" trip. Let us also remember from the words of Nahum about the mercy of God. Even when He corrects us, it is done because of His mercy. The message from Jeremiah is do not allow flesh to dwell within you and then feel comfortable coming into the house of God to praise. Do not be fooled into thinking that because hands are raised that God overlooks the sinfulness of the life we live. Yet, we can rejoice and know that if there is anything in us that needs to be removed, God is the one that can remove it. He has the power over all that would hold us and keep us from being what God has called us to be.

When we go to worship, let's go with a humble heart, seeking God to show us what needs to be laid at the altar, what needs to be released and what needs to be strengthened in us. Let's go having heard, received and willing to live out the living message of God's word. Let's go telling God, I am listening, speak.

Tri-Production Publishing, Inc

Where we Publish the Vision

Helping people WIN in Publishing

To order additional copies of this book visit our website at
https://www.publishthevision.com/

Made in the USA
Columbia, SC
15 November 2022